PUB STROLLS IN
SURREY

David Weller

COUNTRYSIDE BOOKS
NEWBURY BERKSHIRE

First published 2001
© David Weller 2001

COUNTRYSIDE BOOKS
3 Catherine Road
Newbury, Berkshire

To view our complete range of books,
please visit us at
www.countrysidebooks.co.uk

ISBN 1 85306 678 8

Photographs by the author
Maps by the author and redrawn by Techniset Typesetters
Designed by Graham Whiteman

Typeset by Techniset Typesetters, Newton-le-Willows
Produced through MRM Associates Ltd., Reading
Printed by Woolnough Bookbinding Ltd., Irthlingborough

Contents

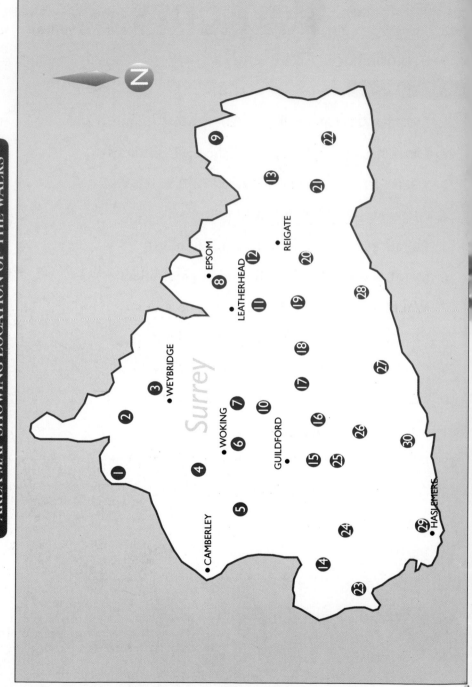

PUBLISHER'S NOTE

We hope that you obtain considerable enjoyment from this book; great care has been taken in its preparation. However, changes of landlord and actual closures are sadly not uncommon. Likewise, although at the time of publication all routes followed public rights of way or permitted paths, diversion orders can be made and permissions withdrawn.

We cannot, of course, be held responsible for such diversion orders and any inaccuracies in the text which result from these or any other changes to the routes nor any damage which might result from walkers trespassing on private property. We are anxious though that all details covering the walks and the pubs are kept up to date and would therefore welcome information from readers which would be relevant to future editions.

The sketch maps accompanying each walk are not always to scale and are intended to guide you to the starting point and give a simple but accurate idea of the route to be taken. For those who like the benefit of detailed maps, we recommend that you arm yourself with the relevant Ordnance Survey map in the Landranger series.

I can think of no better way of spending one's time than strolling through Surrey's prettiest villages and glorious countryside where there is always so much to see and cherish; handsome cottages adorned with roses beside a village green; gaily painted narrow boats negotiating a canal lock; a colourful patchwork of fields bordered by wildflower-filled hedgerows; and cool, peaceful woodland where the sun's rays create dancing patterns on the foliage below.

Throughout each season the spectacle will change. As summer passes into autumn the countryside slows down and glows with golds and browns where the once shady woodland now becomes carpeted by fallen leaves and offers news vistas over the surrounding area. During winter the still waters of a pond may freeze over leaving the ducks sidelined and reed spikes draped with frosted cobwebs that are highlighted by a low watery sun.

Change will also be seen at the village green where the sound of willow striking leather to the lazy handclap of a few spectators gives way to the hoots and howls of a rowdier sport as twenty-two grown men chase through the mud after one ball. Before long spring returns and light breezes send the exquisite perfume of fresh blossom back into the lungs of the countryside where, with new vigour, the cycle starts over again.

Added to this kaleidoscope of pleasures are the splendid hostelries that offer a worthy selection of food, fine ales and most of all a friendly welcome to complement these 30 strolls. The inns and pubs have a charm of their own, perhaps ancient beams, an inglenook fireplace, a highwayman theme or old horse brasses — all adding atmosphere while you enjoy the gastronomic delights each one offers, whether by the warmth of a log fire in winter or at a table in the cool shade of a well-manicured garden during summer. Whatever the season, life's pressures will just drift away over the horizon like an early morning mist.

The easy to follow circular routes pass through a good variety of pretty scenery, from canal towpaths, river banks and rolling pastures to heathland and woodland where the only sound to break the quietness is the delicate sound of birdsong. Ranging from just $1\frac{1}{2}$ miles to 4 miles long there is something for all ages and abilities with each stroll description containing numbered paragraphs that correspond to a simple sketch map. Parking is usually available for patrons at each pub but you should always seek permission from the landlord before leaving your car while you walk; alternatively I have suggested additional parking nearby. For convenience I have included the telephone number of each establishment so that you may check opening times and make bookings for meals in advance if necessary.

All of these easily undertaken strolls are along public rights of way and require no local knowledge or specialist equipment but to add more detail of the areas you pass through I would recommend the Ordnance Survey map quoted with each route. Please always respect the countryside and observe the Country Code at all times, and above all enjoy your stroll.

David Weller

Englefield Green
The Barley Mow

MAP: OS LANDRANGER 176 (GR 992714)   **WALK 1**   **DISTANCE:** 3 MILES

DIRECTIONS TO START: ENGLEFIELD GREEN IS ON THE A328 ABOUT 1½ MILES WEST OF EGHAM.
PARKING: AROUND THE LARGE VILLAGE GREEN

This very pleasant and interesting stroll starts alongside the delightful village green and before long reaches a lovely path that leads us down the magnificent tree-covered slopes of Cooper's Hill to cross Runnymede's water meadows and soon meet the river Thames. The route continues along the water's edge before turning away and re-crossing the famous meadows. It was here during May of 1215 that Stephan Langton acted as mediator between the English barons and the oppressive rule of King John. The King eventually agreed to the barons' demands and signed the momentous document that has become known throughout the world as Magna Carta. This document laid the foundations for English law and liberty that we all take rather for granted. As the route leaves these historic meadows behind we pass along a wonderful cobbled path between trees where we discover the simple block of inscribed Portland stone that forms the John F. Kennedy Memorial from where we make our return back up the slopes of Cooper's Hill to Englefield Green.

The Barley Mow

There is a story told of a duel taking place beween two Frenchmen named Cournet and Barthélemy on Englefield Green during October 1852. Said to be the last duel fought in England it makes a strange tale of chivalry, or could it possibly be stupidity? Cournet won the toss and the choice to fire first but he missed – now it was Barthélemy's turn. He pulled the trigger twice but his pistol failed to fire. Cournet then offered him his own pistol which Barthélemy accepted and he fatally shot Cournet who was carried by his supporters to the Barley Mow where he died a few hours later.

Nowadays this attractive little pub is a quieter place where friendly staff offer ramblers a warm welcome as well as a fine choice of snacks that cover all tastes. Food is available up to 9.30 pm each evening and there is no need to book. From the pumps in the cosy bar come Courage Best, Directors, Theakston Best and a constantly changing guest ale. On my last visit I sat at a table on the sunny patio in the shade of a large umbrella where I enjoyed a leisurely lunch while a game of cricket was being played on the green opposite. Telephone: 01784 431857.

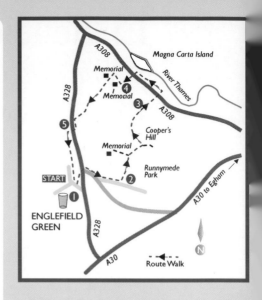

The Walk

① With your back to the Barley Mow, cross the green and head towards a bus stop. Cross the A328 and pass to the right of the bus shelter to reach a road named Middle Hill. Turn right along the road and keep left at a fork and continue along Tite Road.

② Immediately after a road named Kingswood Rise turn left on a footpath that soon goes between gardens. Before long a driveway is met where our way is along the drive to the right. A short excursion of 70 yards or so to your left here brings you to the unusual 'control tower' monument of the Commonwealth Air Forces Memorial. Our way is rightwards passing Kingswood Hall of the University of London. Keep ahead here and, as the drive bends to the right, go left on a well maintained stepped path that leads you down the wooded slopes of Cooper's Hill.

③ At the foot of the slopes continue ahead between meadows and at an open grassy area keep ahead and cross a busy road. Turn right on a grassy path here and soon the bank of the river Thames is met where a couple of welcoming seats make

The Runnymede Memorial.

the perfect picnic spot and mark the halfway point of the stroll. Continue along the river bank until opposite the Runnymede Memorial on your left; re-cross the road and meadow to reach it.

④ From the memorial, turn right along the meadow edge and then left on a signposted path to the JFK memorial. From the inscribed Portland stone memorial press on uphill through woodland to pass a house and keep ahead along a peaceful driveway alongside the picturesque grounds of Brunel University.

⑤ When the A328 is met, turn left along the road and in a short distance as you cross the end of Castle Hill Road continue ahead on a woodland path that runs parallel to the main road. Keep ahead on the main path and soon the expanse of Englefield Green is met where you continue forward to meet up with the Barley Mow and the end of the stroll.

PLACE OF INTEREST NEARBY

Windsor is just 4 miles west of Englefield Green where, apart from seeing the castle, you can take a French Brothers' boat trip along the Thames lasting 35 minutes or 2 hours. Telephone: 01753 851900.

Laleham
The Three Horseshoes

MAP: OS LANDRANGER 176 (GR 052693)   **WALK 2**   **DISTANCE:** 1½ MILES

DIRECTIONS TO START: LALEHAM IS 2 MILES SOUTH-EAST OF THE CENTRE OF STAINES ALONG THE B376. YOU WILL FIND THE THREE HORSESHOES JUST SOUTH OF A TIGHT BEND BY THE CHURCH.
PARKING: IN THE PUB CAR PARK OR ALONG THE B376.

Laleham is such a joy to explore as the village has a wealth of old cottages in hidden lanes away from the constant flow of today's traffic on the B376. Within yards of the start we cross the road by the old church which is mostly Norman and stroll down Blacksmith's Lane where pretty cottages line the road. Soon the route reaches the river Thames where we follow its bank westwards to reach Penton Hook Lock where we can sit and watch the river traffic passing through its gates. For the return to Laleham we retrace our steps back along the river bank to meet up with Ferry Lane from where we return to the centre of the village.

This stroll is ideal for those with a wheelchair or pushchair as the route is level and hard surfaced. For those with a little more energy the stroll can be extended by a further couple of miles by continuing along the river bank towards Staines.

The Three Horseshoes

The Three Horseshoes has the distinction of having had one of the longest serving licensees in Surrey's pub history. William Clifton's stewardship of the pub ended in 1925 after he had held the post for over forty years. I wonder what he would think if he could return today. From the pumps come Directors, Bombadier and John Smith's bitters, Carlsberg and Foster's lagers, plus Guinness and Dry Blackthorn cider. Food is served 11 am to 2 pm on weekdays only. The last time I visited the Three Horseshoes it was one of those lovely late summer days when the temperature was still high enough to allow one to sit in the very pleasant garden area. No matter what time of the year you call in you will find a warm and friendly welcome in the comfortable bar. Being not too far from the banks of the Thames makes this a popular little spot, but never mind it is still worth the visit even if you have to share its popularity with others. Telephone: 020 8890 2463.

② Turn right here along a broad path that follows the river bank while to your right are houses with unequalled views of the river. Before long a small road is met and our route continues along it with the river close by.

③ It is not long before you find yourself alongside Penton Hook Lock and Weirs. There are seats here which make this a very pleasant place to pass some time watching the boats negotiate the lock. You may of course extend the stroll by continuing along the river bank a further mile or two if you really want to stretch

The Walk

① Turn right out of the Three Horseshoes and within yards you pass the early 18th century Dial House with its unique sundial. Continue alongside the road until you meet the tight bend by the old church. With caution cross the road and pass the war memorial and enter Blacksmith's Lane where you press on to very soon reach the bank of the Thames.

PLACE OF INTEREST NEARBY

Sited 3 miles east of Laleham on the A308 is **Sunbury Park Walled Garden** which contains both an Elizabethan knot garden and a Victorian rose garden. Open daily all year from 11 am to 5 pm. **Spelthorne Museum** is housed in the old fire station near the Town Hall in Staines. Open Wednesdays and Fridays from 2 pm to 4 pm and 1.30 pm to 4.30 pm on Saturdays. Telephone: 01784 461804.

The magnificent sundial on Dial House.

your legs. Our route retraces our steps from the lock back along the river bank. When Blacksmith's Lane is reached do not turn left into it but continue ahead alongside the river.

④ After passing more houses that overlook the river you come to Ferry Lane on the left. Turn left here to reach the B376 opposite the Three Horsehoes, neatly ending the stroll.

Shepperton
The Kings Head

MAP: OS LANDRANGER 176 (GR 076667)   **WALK 3**   DISTANCE: 2½ MILES

DIRECTIONS TO START: FROM SOUTH OF THE THAMES CROSS THE RIVER AT WALTON-ON-THAMES AND TURN LEFT ON THE B375. AT A ROUNDABOUT GO LEFT INTO CHURCH ROAD AND SOON LEFT AGAIN INTO CHURCH SQUARE. **PARKING:** VERY LIMITED AT THE PUB SO USE THE FREE CAR PARK OFF CHURCH ROAD.

Shepperton sits at the confluence of the rivers Wey, Bourne and Thames and was a part of the county of Middlesex until the town planners decided to change the border in 1965. The gain was Surrey's as this age-old village makes a superb place to explore. At its heart is Church Square, a real gem where the Kings Head pub and a couple of hotels frame the lovely church while just a stone's throw away is the bank of the Thames.

Our stroll is level and mostly along tarmac surfaces making it mud free after heavy rain and ideal for those with a wheelchair or pushchair. The route heads down Ferry Lane to meet the Thames at Shepperton Lock where pleasure craft will be seen passing through its gates. After following the river bank for a mile our return route is along a couple of roads that bring us back to Church Square and the end of this easy stroll.

The Kings Head

Not a lot has changed in this lovely old coaching inn for the last 500 years. The horse-drawn traffic may have given way to the motor car and aeroplanes now fly overhead but enter this tiny pub with its low ceilings and ancient oak beams and be cast back to those far off days when people such as Nell Gwyn and Charles II are said to have come here. More recently, Elizabeth Taylor and the late Richard Burton as well as other celebrities have visited while filming at the world famous Shepperton Studios nearby.

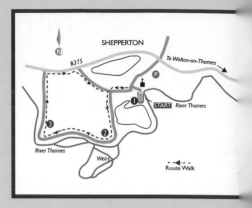

This delightful little pub sits in picturesque Church Square and hides behind its sumptuous window boxes that are a riot of colour during the summer months. It is a free house and serves Courage Best, Directors and Theakston Best bitters from the pump with a good selection of wines by the glass or bottle. An ever changing variety of delicious pub food covering most tastes including vegetarian is available between 12 noon and 2.15 pm and between 7 pm and 9.30 pm on weekdays, 12 noon and 2.15 pm only on Saturdays and sadly not at all for those visiting on Sundays. Telephone: 01932 221910.

The Walk

① If you parked in the free car park in Manor Park then go out to Church Road and turn left to soon meet up with Church Square and the Kings Head. If you did manage to park in Church Square then walk back to Church Road. Our route continues leftwards along Chertsey Road where before long we turn left into Ferry Lane and continue until the Thames is reached.

② Upon meeting the river turn right and continue along the bank where you soon pass Shepperton Lock. Our route now passes a variety of homes that have grown over the years from basic wooden cabins into what can best be described as architecturally 'individual'. Another mixture of houses of varying sizes can be seen to your left on Pharaoh's Island where each has its own private mooring at the garden edge. One motor cruiser I saw moored there was actually larger than the house.

PLACE OF INTEREST NEARBY

Claremont Garden contains 50 acres of landscaped grounds that were designed in the 18th century but later became overgrown and unkempt. Now restored to their former glory by the National Trust the grounds include a lake, grotto, temple, belvedere and bowling green. The gardens are 1 mile south of Esher on the A307. Opening times vary. Telephone: 01372 469421.

A peaceful scene on the Thames.

③ The halfway mark of our stroll comes just before the road heads away from the river bank and if you find that leaving the water's edge is too much to bear then you could of course retrace your steps from here. Continuing the circuit we press on along the lane to meet a T-junction with the B375. Turn right alongside the road and soon after passing the entrance to Mead Farm turn right into Chertsey Road. Press on along the road and pass by Ferry Lane where you now retrace your steps back to the Kings Head and the end of our stroll.

Chobham
The Sun Inn

MAP: OS LANDRANGER 186 (GR 974618) | **WALK 4** | **DISTANCE:** 2 MILES

DIRECTIONS TO START: CHOBHAM IS 3 MILES NORTH OF WOKING AT THE JUNCTION OF THE A3046 AND A319. **PARKING:** IN THE PUB CAR PARK OR IN THE FREE CAR PARK AT THE NORTH END OF THE HIGH STREET.

Chobham's quiet High Street contains many 18th century buildings that are now converted to antique shops and eateries making it an interesting place to explore. This easy and level stroll starts at the mid point of the village opposite the 11th century church and continues south along a residential road where we soon cross The Bourne stream. As our route swings eastwards we enter woodland and re-cross the stream as the circular route makes its way to another of Chobham's small waterways, the Mill Bourne. Here the route shadows the clear running waters where on a warm summer's day there can be no finer place to stroll in the whole of Surrey than these hay meadows where the air becomes perfumed by the drifts of balsam that crowd the water's edge. Soon we find ourselves back in the High Street where we pass a Russian 24-pound cannon displaying itself at Cannon Corner, a reminder of less peaceful times and of Chobham's link with the army.

The Sun Inn

The Sun Inn is one of Surrey's old coaching inns dating back to the 15th century and apart from St Lawrence's church opposite there is not a lot in Chobham that is older. Set in the middle of the High Street the inn still retains its olde worlde charm despite the ever increasing through traffic that passes its door. The cosy bar has exposed beams, as you would expect, but there is one oddity that is a surprise – an old telephone box that now finds use as a wine store. I can highly recommend relaxing by the warmth of an open log fire as the flames warm you after a pleasant winter stroll over the surrounding countryside. From the pumps comes a good selection of beers including Courage Best, Directors, Becketts Stoke Ale, Pedigree and Ringwood, plus Carlsberg, Kronenbourg, Grolsch and Foster's lagers. Sup your ale in comfort and enjoy a good meal freshly cooked by the friendly staff. During the summer months there are tables with brightly coloured umbrellas set up outside on the patio area where you can sit and watch the world go by. It is always advisable to book a table if you wish to eat a sit down meal here. Food is served from 12 noon to 2.30 pm and from 7.30 pm to 9.30 pm every day. Telephone: 01276 857112.

The Walk

① If you have parked in the free car park then go out to the car park entrance and turn left along the road where you pass Cannon Corner. Keep ahead and walk along the pleasant High Street and soon pass the Sun Inn to meet a mini roundabout. If you are starting from the Sun Inn then turn right along the High Street to meet the mini roundabout. Keep ahead along Castle Grove Road to soon cross The Bourne stream and before long turn left into Broadford Lane. Whilst this is not the prettiest lane in Chobham it does offer easy walking and plenty of birdlife in the adjoining hedgerows. Eventually turn left on a bridleway just before gates are met. Here we re-cross The Bourne and make our way along a path through a ribbon of woodland that brings us to a shingle driveway where we continue ahead to meet a road.

② Cross the road and press on diagonally right along Sandpit Hall Road where, after about 200 yards, you should cross a stile on your left alongside Willow Tree House. At a field edge cross a stile and another ahead of you beside a field gate. Press on ahead along the right-hand field edge to meet another stile on your right but do not cross it. From here follow an indistinct path diagonally leftwards over the field to meet yet another stile ahead of you in trees.

③ After crossing the stile keep ahead and at the far side of the meadow you will meet a T-junction with a small path with the Mill Bourne flowing behind it. Turn

PLACE OF INTEREST NEARBY

Chobham Common is one of our National Nature Reserves and is just 2 miles to the north of the village. This wonderfully invigorating piece of heathland is one of the largest in the south-east and is a pleasure to explore. No information centre but several car parks.

Cannon Corner, Chobham.

left here and keep to this very pleasant meadow path as it follows the stream. Eventually, when the path can no longer follow the stream, it swings leftwards and very soon you should turn right on a fenced path alongside the free car park. For those who parked their car here then this is the end of the stroll. For those who started at the pub, turn left at the road to pass Cannon Corner and continue ahead to soon meet up with the Sun Inn.

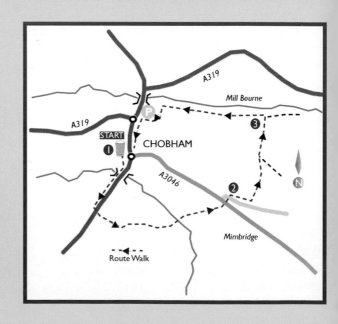

Pirbright
The Cricketers Inn

MAP: OS LANDRANGER 186 (GR 947559)   **WALK 5**   **DISTANCE:** 2 MILES

DIRECTIONS TO START: PIRBRIGHT IS ON THE A324 SOME 4½ MILES TO THE NORTH-WEST OF GUILDFORD. THE PUB IS ALONGSIDE THE GREEN BY THE VILLAGE POND. **PARKING:** IN THE PUB CAR PARK OR IN PARKING AREAS AROUND THE VILLAGE GREEN.

The charming village of Pirbright stands on the very edge of armydom and is not in the least bit spoiled by the closeness. Elegant houses and a couple of old pubs edge the well-manicured village green that has an airy look about it. There is a peaceful pond where children can feed the ducks and further away are well-used football and cricket pitches. The route leaves this scene by pretty Church Lane where we pass a large granite obelisk marking the grave of Sir Henry Morton Stanley in St Michael's churchyard. Inscribed 'Bula Matari' – the African name for him – this spot marks the final resting place of the much travelled journalist and explorer. Before long our way crosses pleasant verdant pastures to meet another quiet lane where the route passes the site of an old watermill. More meadows follow before we find ourselves back at St Michael's from where we return to the village green.

The Cricketers Inn

This lovely hostelry is almost opposite the village pond and is thought to date as far back as the 17th century. The signage painted on the front wall cleverly disguises that a window has been blocked in, probably to lessen the effect of Pitt's window tax imposed during the 18th century. The much later side additions are fine and fail to spoil the overall pleasant look of the inn as so many new extensions generally do. Pass through the door and you find yourself entering a typical Surrey village pub, friendly and welcoming, functional, and none too fussy.

From the pumps in the cosy bar come London Pride, Killkenny, Guinness and Adnams ales plus a fair selection of wines by the glass or bottle. During the summer months the secluded garden is a haven for families who enjoy the agreeable village atmosphere while their children play happily in the area set aside for them. Food is available from 12 noon until 2 pm every day and on my last visit I thoroughly enjoyed a splendid ploughman's lunch – on hot days I much prefer the big chunks of cheese, lashings of pickle and good crusty bread to something cooked. Booking is essential on Sundays. Telephone: 01483 473198.

The Walk

① From the Cricketers Inn go left and pass the village pond. Go diagonally half right across the corner of the green to meet and cross the A324. Our route is along Church Lane opposite, where, at a

bend in the road, we see the granite obelisk marking Stanley's grave in St Michael's churchyard. It's amazing how his four words 'Dr Livingstone I presume' have endured time and are known around the world.

② Soon after passing the church with its golden dragon weather vane, go left over a stile beside a field gate and continue along the left side of two fields. Cross a stile and press on along an enclosed path to reach Mill Lane. Turn right along the lane where you will soon pass an old millstone set in a hedge by the entrance to Mill House. From the lane you will see a leat and a millpond on this old watermill site. Press on along this little lane that offers fine shade on a hot summer's day.

The sound of far off gunfire is commonplace in the Pirbright area as our army practises at their distant firing ranges. Perhaps I should mention, though, at this point that just occasionally it can sound as if World War III has broken out when a field firing range only $\frac{1}{2}$ mile away to the west is used.

③ Soon after passing the entrance to Pirbright Lodge keep right at a fork and at a second fork turn right on an uphill footpath by holly trees. Now keep ahead with a fence on your right and soon cross a stile. Continue over a field towards a

The granite obelisk in St Michael's churchyard.

kissing gate opposite then continue over the next field and pass through another kissing gate. Follow the path leftwards and very soon cross a bridge over the Hodge Brook. Follow the path along a ribbon of trees and soon meet up with Church Lane.

④ Turn right along the lane and 20 yards after passing the entrance to Appletree Farm seek out a stile in the bank on your right. Cross this and follow the left-hand field edge to meet a field gate by a stile we crossed earlier. Go out to Church Lane and continue to the right where we retrace out steps back to the Cricketers Inn and the end of the stroll.

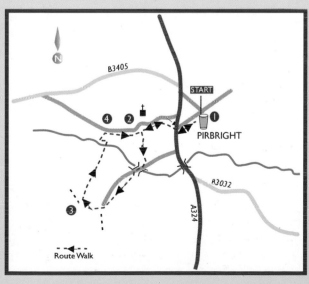

Sutton Green
The Fox and Hounds

MAP: OS LANDRANGER 186 (GR 006545)   **WALK 6**   **DISTANCE:** 3 MILES

DIRECTIONS TO START: SUTTON GREEN CAN BE FOUND ½ MILE EAST OF THE A320 MIDWAY BETWEEN GUILDFORD AND WOKING.. **PARKING:** IN THE PUB CAR PARK OR ALONG SUTTON GREEN ROAD.

The small community of Sutton Green is rather linear and, contrary to its name, has no village green and therefore lacks a focal point. Our route takes us to the idyllic towpath of the Wey Navigation where its lush growth of vegetation and panoramic views across the water meadows to St Mary's church at Send Grove make this a most pleasurable scene. Take your time here for there is a host of things to see as the route follows the towpath through this tranquil little piece of Surrey; narrow boats negotiating a lock, wildflowers at the canal margin, elegant damselflies flying over the water and the occasional spatter of a fish as it seizes a mosquito from the mirror-like surface of the canal. Leaving here we return through peaceful meadows with hedgerows embellished with flowers during summer before the route rejoins the canal bank and we retrace our steps back to the village and the end of our stroll.

The Fox and Hounds

Sitting at the southern end of the village of Sutton Green is the popular Fox and Hounds public house. Contemporary to most of the houses that are strung out along the road here, this very pleasant hostelry offers a warm welcome to all who visit. This is a pub of contrasts as at one end of the longish bar is a pool table where younger folk tend to gather while the bar proper offers the usual traditional comforts and down two steps in a newer extended part is a very nice cottage-style dining area with an open fire on cold days.

Food is available from 12 noon to 2 pm and 6 pm to 9 pm on weekdays and Saturdays while on Sundays it is available from 12 noon until 7 pm. The extensive menu offers anything from fish and chips, chicken tikka masala, a huge mixed grill and even a vegetarian version of sausage and mash. I particularly enjoyed the tuna and cheese melt which was filling enough to satisfy the largest of appetites. Look out for the 'specials' blackboard with the chef's daily choice. From the pumps come Bass, Tetley's Smooth, Grolsch, Carlsberg and Guinness and there is a selection of red and white wines by the glass or bottle. Booking on Sundays is recommended. Telephone: 01483 772289.

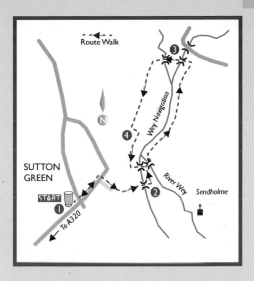

The Walk

① From the Fox and Hounds turn left along the road to very soon meet a road junction. Keep ahead along a quiet residential lane and immediately after passing a bungalow named Compton turn right on a footpath along the drive to Wareham's Farm. At the end of the drive press on ahead passing large barns. Soon go left on a waymarked public footpath to reach and cross a small bridge over the Wey Navigation.

② Turn left here and continue along the picturesque towpath where you pass Triggs Lock and the quaint lock keeper's cottage. Press on alongside the towpath and pass Worsfold Gates, a lock with a rise of only a few inches. Soon you pass houses to meet a driveway where you should now turn left over a narrow footbridge.

PLACE OF INTEREST NEARBY
Situated in Clay Lane in nearby Jacob's Well is **Burpham Court Farm Park**, set in 77 acres of beautiful countryside with the river Wey at its heart. Picnic with the rare breeds of cattle, sheep, goats, pigs and pets. Open 10 am to 6 pm every day from February to October. Telephone: 01483 576089.

A narrowboat negotiating Triggs Lock.

③ Pass by wrought iron gates to meet a concrete drive where you continue ahead and left to soon cross a small stream. Before long the drive crosses the river Wey and ends by a house. Turn left over a stile here and press on along a peaceful grassy farm track alongside a hazel hedge where during late summer a veritable feast of cob nuts display themselves.

④ Eventually you should go left over a stile just before reaching farm buildings. Keep to the grassy track as it skirts the farm and meets a second stile. Cross this to join a farm track and now turn left to very soon re-cross the Wey Navigation. Turn right along the canal and go right again over the next bridge to retrace your steps back to the village and the end of the stroll.

Ripley
The Talbot Hotel

| MAP: OS LANDRANGER 187 (GR 055569) | **WALK 7** | DISTANCE: 2¼ MILES |

DIRECTIONS TO START: RIPLEY IS JUST OFF THE A3 A MILE SOUTH OF JUNCTION 10 OF THE M25. THE TALBOT HOTEL IS AT THE EASTERN END OF THE HIGH STREET. **PARKING:** IN THE PUB CAR PARK OR ALONGSIDE THE VILLAGE GREEN.

Ripley sits on the old Portsmouth Road and was once an important staging post for coaches passing between London and Portsmouth. Lying hidden behind the High Street is Ripley's huge green where cricket has been played for over 200 years. The locals boast that this is Surrey's largest village green and they could well be right. Our route passes over this airy area and meets the river Wey and the Wey Navigation by Walsham Lock. Here we follow the scenic towpath awhile where narrow boats, now without their cargoes, ply the waters with pleasure seekers. Soon we re-cross the river and pass a lovely cluster of houses by Ockham Mill. Built in 1862 on an ancient mill site the impressive building has been converted to handsome living accommodation. Leaving here we pass through peaceful woodland to again meet up with the grassy expanse of Ripley green and the end of the stroll.

The Talbot Hotel

The austere Georgian frontage of the Talbot Hotel tries its hardest to disguise the inn's origins but the façade is only skin deep for as you pass under the arched entrance-way you are transported back to the early days of this lovely 15th century coaching inn. Half close your eyes and you can almost see Lord Nelson and Lady Hamilton's horse-drawn carriage being driven through the arch some two hundred and fifty years ago for they are among the inn's distinguished guest list.

The courtyard now contains tables and chairs where patrons sit under gaily coloured umbrellas in the summer sun while the outbuildings now house an antiques centre making this pub a truly fascinating place to visit. Inside, the cosy bar has, as you would expect, low ceilings and old beams and plenty of atmosphere. From the pumps come Greene King IPA, Flowers Original, Courage Best, Boddingtons, Guinness, Stella, Heineken, Hoegaarden and Dry Blackthorn cider, a much broader choice of drinks than Nelson would have been offered. A good selection of bar food is always available, but if you are looking for something special then try the Emma Hamilton Restaurant where varied three-course meals are on offer from the à la carte menu. Food is served from 12 noon to 3 pm and from 7 pm to 9.30 pm Monday to Saturday; and on Sunday from 12 noon to 2 pm only. (Sunday booking essential). Telephone: 01483 225188.

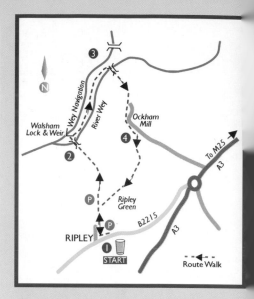

The Walk

① From the Talbot Hotel cross the High Street and go left for around 100 yards or so and then turn right along a small lane that takes you past additional parking and the attractive cricket pitch. Continue on this lane as it runs along the edge of the green and passes houses. Follow it leftwards at a bend and soon cross Ockham millstream. Within yards the lane ends and you should go ahead on a waymarked path by a holly bush. Cross fields to reach the weir at Walsham Lock.

② Cross the rushing waters of the weir and turn right along the Wey Navigation, passing the lock keeper's cottage. Our route lies ahead along the towpath of the

PLACE OF INTEREST NEARBY

Wisley Garden (Royal Horticultural Society) is world famous for its flowering displays. Just off the A3 north of Ripley, it is open from Monday to Saturday between 10 am and 7 pm in summer or 4.30 pm during winter. Telephone: 01483 224234.

The Wey Navigation.

canal where narrow boats moor on the opposite bank. The Wey Navigation was built in 1653 by Sir Richard Weston of Sutton Place and was the first river to be improved or 'canalised' in England, becoming navigable from the Thames at Weybridge as far as Guildford by the building of 12 locks.

③ About 300 yards before a bridge is met go right at a post on a path that leads you through woodland to Ockham Mill. The millstream we crossed earlier in the stroll was cut by hand to drive this and earlier mills that occupied the site.

④ Press on along the lane and very soon you pass a post-box half-hidden in a hedge to your right. Just after passing this go right on a path and cross a small wooden bridge where you now continue through peaceful woodland. After crossing a second wooden bridge keep ahead through the trees to meet the expanse of Ripley green. Remain on a well-trodden path through a fine mixture of tall grasses that sway in the breeze. It's pleasing to see that not all villages feel the need to fulfil today's penchant for close cropping by over zealous mower blades.

Epsom Downs
The Derby Arms

MAP: OS LANDRANGER 187 (GR 217587)   **WALK 8**   **DISTANCE:** 2 MILES

DIRECTIONS TO START: FROM THE CENTRE OF EPSOM HIGH STREET GO SOUTH ALONG ASHLEY ROAD (B290). WHEN AT EPSOM DOWNS BY THE GRANDSTAND GO LEFT AT THE ROUNDABOUT AND LEFT AGAIN TO REACH THE DERBY ARMS. **PARKING:** IN THE PUB CAR PARK OR ALONG VERGES.

Thousands of excited race-goers flock to Epsom Downs each year to witness the horse-racing which includes two of the most famous races on earth, the Derby and the Oaks. Very fortunately for us the downs have seen it all before and soon after the crowds have dispersed they return to their much cherished and breezy ways. The whole of the course and downs are open for all to freely roam when there are no race meetings so pick your day carefully. This easy stroll takes in stunning views over the London skyline before turning south and crossing the famous turf by Tattenham Corner. As we meet up with Walton Downs our route turns northward through woodland and soon re-crosses the race course. Near the end of the stroll we pass close to the distinctive grandstands and all too soon find ourselves back at the Derby Arms and the end of the stroll.

The Derby Arms

I remember years ago when the Derby Arms was not much larger than a double-fronted house and was somewhat overshadowed by the nearby Rubbing Rooms public house that is sited within the race course itself. Since those days the pub has over doubled in size and is much the better for it. Its signage proudly proclaims that it serves 'great British food all day every day' and it has now gained a growing reputation as an eatery. Owned by the Bass brewery under the name of Vintage Inns the pub offers an extensive range of food from lunchtime and evening menus that change with the seasons.

Food is served between 12 noon and 10 pm for six days and until 9 pm on Sundays. I thoroughly enjoyed the roasted vegetable ravioli with basil sauce and Pecorino cheese while others at the table tucked into plates of Three Shires sausage and Cheddar mash served with garlic, bacon and mushroom gravy. There are also smaller platters on offer such as Caesar salad and mixed mushrooms on garlic toast. From the pumps comes a good range of drinks including Bass, Tetley's, Calders, Carlsberg Export, Guinness and Dry Blackthorn cider. At the rear and side of the pub is a lovely large garden where during the summer months you can enjoy your refreshment whilst looking at the London skyline and spotting the individual buildings of our capital city. Telephone: 01372 722330.

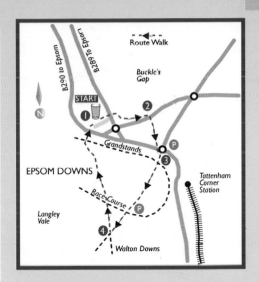

The Walk

① Come out of the Derby Arms and go left over a grassy area to meet up with the roundabout. Cross the road and press on ahead along a grassy cart track that remains parallel with the left side of the road signposted to Burgh Heath and Reigate. From this track on clear days you will have magnificent views over London.

② After passing a couple of parking areas you will meet a stony crossing path. Turn right here, cross the road and press on ahead on the path opposite that goes over a golf course fairway and continues

PLACE OF INTEREST NEARBY
Horton Park Farm in Horton Lane 1 mile west of Epsom is a children's farm where the animals can be fed and stroked. It has an adventure playground, craft shop and refreshment area. Open daily all year from 10 am to 5 pm in winter and until 6 pm in summer. Telephone: 01372 743984.

The famous Epsom racecourse.

through a small piece of woodland. After exiting the woodland press on ahead to meet a road and a small roundabout.

③ Cross the road and continue ahead on a track that crosses the famous turf strip by Tattenham Corner. Our route is now along the chalky track ahead of you that cuts across the middle of the course. At the far side press on ahead over the race track and along a wide dusty cart track.

④ In a short while a junction of tracks is met and you should turn sharp right here and continue through woodland. Press on over the race track to meet a tarmac drive. Keep ahead on this drive as it takes you towards the grandstands in the distance. The contrasting architecture of these grandstands is quite interesting and reflects technological change. The stand to the right of the group was built in 1927 and was the first of its kind to be made from reinforced concrete but unfortunately its fine lines are now totally spoiled by the scourge of our times, a mass of radio aerials. The rather more modern Queen's Stand to the left of it is a creation in glass designed to resemble a two-masted ship while my favourite is the brick-built and perfectly proportioned small Victorian stand of 1879 sited on its own to the left of the group. Eventually pass the front of the Rubbing Rooms public house and cross the racetrack. Bear off right here along a tarmac path and soon cross a road via pedestrian lights. Keep ahead and within yards you will be back at the Derby Arms and the end of the stroll.

Chelsham
The Bull Inn

DIRECTIONS TO START: CHELSHAM IS 5 MILES SOUTH-EAST OF CROYDON AND $\frac{1}{2}$ MILE EAST OF THE B269 AT WARLINGHAM. **PARKING:** IN THE PUB CAR PARK OR AROUND THE GREEN.

The small outlying hamlet of Chelsham nestles against the borders of Greater London and Kent in the far north-eastern corner of Surrey. There is no actual village nucleus, only a loose collection of houses surrounding a small triangular common with the Bull Inn at its centre. This area above the North Downs has become a ramblers' paradise and it's not hard to see why for our route is level, easy to follow and surprisingly rural being this close to Croydon and Greater London. The first part of the stroll takes us alongside woodland and over fields to the south of Chelsham before we head back to the common where the shorter stroll ends. For those with another mile in them we continue northwards where we pass along a wide, easy track through the dappled shade of Holt Wood before returning to the Bull Inn and the end of the stroll.

The Bull Inn

Standing in the middle of Chelsham Common and surrounded by unspoilt countryside is the popular Punch Taverns owned Bull Inn. As you enter the bar, the mouth-watering aroma of home cooking entices you to study the menu where a sumptuous choice of wholesome food is on display including a vegetarian selection. It is served daily from 12 noon to 4 pm and 6 pm to 10 pm or until 9.30 pm on Sundays and the renown of this very popular pub makes booking essential if you wish to dine here. Make yourself at home in the comfortable bar where the real ale enthusiast can sample the constantly changing guest ale from the pumps as well as favourites such as Greene King IPA and Abbot, Harveys Sussex and London Pride ales. If that is not enough choice for you then why not try the Guinness or the Blackthorn or Strongbow ciders, Grolsch, Stella Artois and Carling Black Label lager. This family orientated pub has a large beer garden where you can soak up the summer sun and children have their own play area. I found it quite a task to tear myself away from the comforts of this pleasant pub after my enjoyable lunch. Telephone: 01883 622970.

The Walk

① With the Bull Inn behind you go left through the pub car park to reach the open common. Turn left here and continue on a well-worn path that runs parallel to a road. When the path meets

the road ignore a footpath on your right and continue along the road. Look out for a bridleway beside a gate 10 yards or so before you meet a small road junction. Our route is along this broad pleasant track that borders woodland, with a large field to your left.

② This level track eventually ends at a country lane. Turn right along it to soon meet the B269. Turn right again here and continue alongside the road. At a bus stop opposite a small roadside pond turn right on a well-signposted path to soon cross a stile at a field edge. Keep straight ahead through this field aiming at a marker post on the far side.

PLACE OF INTEREST NEARBY

Titsey Place and Gardens is located just north of Limpsfield off Water Lane. The house has many outstanding features and is set within extensive formal and informal gardens. Open 1 pm to 5 pm on Wednesdays, Sundays and summer bank holidays from the end of May to the end of September. Telephone: 01273 407056.

Our path through the fields.

③ Pass the marker post and cross a stile where you keep ahead through the centre of another field to reach woodland. Very shortly at a field edge, ignore a stile to your right and continue ahead outside the field on a woodland path. Maintain direction through this band of woodland until a T-junction is met with a broader track. Turn right here to soon meet a road.

④ Turn right and walk along the road where you will soon see the welcoming Bull Inn and the end of the shorter stroll. If you wish to resist the pub's pleasures for a little while longer then bear left alongside the common and pass a telephone box. Keep ahead at a small road junction and continue along what was the drive to the former Warlingham Park Hospital.

⑤ At the end of the drive continue ahead along a narrow tarmac path and soon fork left by an oak tree. After passing through peaceful woodland cross a stile at a field edge and keep ahead on the right-hand field edge. Cross a second stile and, ignoring another ahead of you, turn right along the wide track. Keep to this lovely track as it leads you through Holt Wood and eventually meets a road. Turn right along the road for a short distance to again meet up with the common and the end of the stroll.

Martyr's Green
The Black Swan

MAP: OS LANDRANGER 187 (GR 090573)   **WALK 10**   **DISTANCE:** $2\frac{3}{4}$ MILES

DIRECTIONS TO START: MARTYR'S GREEN IS $\frac{3}{4}$ MILE NORTH-EAST OF OCKHAM ALONG OCKHAM LANE
THE BLACK SWAN IS AT THE CROSSROADS WITH OLD LANE. **PARKING:** IN THE PUB CAR PARK OR
ALONG VERGES.

This interesting stroll is through lovely countryside bounded by both the A3 and the M25, but neither interferes with our pleasure. Martyr's Green contains little more than the excellent Black Swan pub and a few outlying cottages so apart from the gastronomic delights of this fine hostelry our interest must lie elsewhere. The route has a theme based on signalling and soon, as we go over a field, we pass a flying-saucer shaped radio beacon that pinpoints to passing aircraft their position. Within yards we find ourselves crossing the disused runway of Wisley Airfield, once the British Aircraft Corporation's communications test centre. Heading north through heathland we reach Chatley Heath where we discover an old semaphore tower amongst the serene pine trees. Built in 1822 when the memory of the Napoleonic Wars was still fresh in the Government's mind, this tower was one of a line that sent messages back and forth from the Admiralty in London to the naval dockyard at Portsmouth.

The Black Swan

The Black Swan has the sort of look about it that has attracted many film makers to use it in scenes ranging from *American Werewolf in London* to episodes of *Inspector Morse* and numerous adverts and no doubt the stars availed themselves of the superb facilities. As well as being popular with the film industry this is the ideal pub for the whole family to visit as during the summer months you can sit in the sunny garden while your children exhaust themselves on the bouncy castle in the play area. On selected weekends there is also a barbecue which always proves popular. If you prefer to sit inside or call in during the winter months you can make yourself at home in the comfortable bar or restaurant.

A good range of food that includes a vegetarian selection and a choice for children is on offer from 12 noon to 2.30 pm and 6.30 pm to 9.30 pm on weekdays, 12 noon to 9.30 pm on Saturdays and 12 noon to 8 pm on Sundays, and there is no need to book. Being a freehouse means there is a huge selection of thirst quenchers on offer including Caffrey's, Guinness, John Smith's, Carling, Foster's, Holsten, Kronenbourg and Strongbow cider, plus fourteen real ales on tap. How's that for choice? Telephone: 01932 862364.

The Walk

① With the Black Swan behind you, cross the road and walk along Ockham Lane. Soon after passing the entrance to Upton Farm and going round a left bend in the

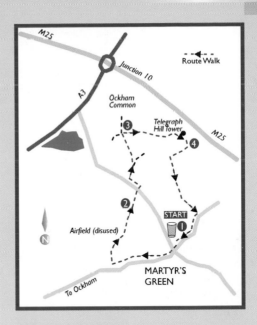

road cross a stile in the right-hand bank. Press on up a slope and go over two further stiles to reach a fingerpost by the side of a large field. Cross the field on a well-used path to the left of a radio beacon and soon reach the disused runway of Wisley Airfield. I remember back in the mid 1960s watching jet airliners take off and land here in this quiet little place. Press

PLACE OF INTEREST NEARBY

The **semaphore tower at Chatley Heath** is open from the end of March to the beginning of October from 12 noon to 5 pm on Saturdays, Sundays and bank holidays plus Wednesdays during school holidays, also some Sundays in the winter months. A small admission fee is charged. Telephone: 01932 862762. The Royal Horticultural Society's magnificent **Wisley Garden** is just off the A3 one mile south of junction 10 of the M25. Open all year on Monday to Saturday from 10 am to 7 pm in summer and 4.30 pm in winter. Closed to non-members on Sundays. Telephone: 01483 224234.

The old semaphore tower on Chatley Heath.

When the bridlewa[y] forks keep to th[e] left fork.

③ At a large junctio[n] of tracks by a pos[t] with a red marke[r] arrow turn righ[t] Soon, look out for [a] second red marke[r] post directing yo[u] rightwards along [a] smaller track. No[w] follow the red arro[w] marker posts to reac[h] the old semaphor[e] tower and a pleasan[t] picnic area with tables and seats.

④ Our way continues to the right of the tower for a few yards along a driveway. When the drive soon turns to the left go right here on a pleasing downward sloping bridleway between rhododendrons and chestnut trees. At a large junction of tracks by a fingerpost turn left along a bridleway signposted to Ockham Lane. Ignore side paths and stay ahead on the main track to reach a large open grassy area where you should continue ahead along a quiet track to reach Ockham Lane. When the road is reached turn right along it to soon meet the Black Swan pub and the end of the stroll.

on over the runway to the path opposite and maintain direction ahead.

② At the end of the field continue along the left side of a row of old oak trees and cross two stiles in succession to the right of a house before pressing on to reach a road. Turn left along the road for a short distance and then turn right onto a bridleway beside Surrey Cottage.

Mickleham
The Running Horses

DIRECTIONS TO START: MICKLEHAM IS SITUATED 3 MILES NORTH OF DORKING JUST OFF THE A24 ON THE B2209 OLD LONDON ROAD. **PARKING:** ALONG THE B2209.

Thankfully Mickleham was bypassed by the A24 long ago and looks much better for it as today's traffic has no place in such a quaint little spot as this. The squat Norman church tower, pretty village store, post office and the 16th century Running Horses pub make this village such a delight. After leaving the village behind, the route passes through fields and over the river Mole to reach Westhumble before steadily climbing 300 feet up the valley side in a not too strenuous ascent. The reward for this effort is worthwhile though as from a viewpoint in Norbury Park you will discover a couple of seats where you are able to observe the pretty Mole Valley laid out below you. The route now descends through Norbury Park to reach the open hillside and then re-crosses the river Mole to soon return to Mickleham and the Running Horses.

The Running Horses

The pub owes its name to the Epsom Derby of 1828 which produced a dead-heat between *Cadland* and *The Colonel*. One side of the sign shows both horses while on the other is shown *The Colonel*, the winner of the re-run race a few days later. The pub is much older and has attracted customers from far and wide for over 400 years and you will see just why. During cold winter days you will be warmed by the blazing log fire in the inglenook fireplace and when you reach for the menu you will find such delicacies as 'Rustic Smoked Bacon and Chicken Liver Paté served with Plum Chutney and Warm Bread'. Summer brings a totally different atmosphere as tables under colourful umbrellas line the pavement outside and we sit and watch the world go by in this quiet and peaceful village.

As well as a good choice of bar food, the establishment boasts a fine English restaurant where you can savour the excellent cuisine that will satisfy all tastes. From the pumps come bitters such as London Pride, Young's Best, King & Barnes Sussex, Friary Meaux Best Bitter, Old Speckled Hen plus a constantly changing guest ale while a good selection of wine can be purchased by the glass or bottle. This is a very popular pub and you must book in advance if you wish to eat in the restaurant. Food is served from 12 noon to 2.30 pm and 7 pm to 9.30 pm Monday to Saturday; and on Sunday from 12 noon to 2.30 pm only. Telephone: 01372 372279.

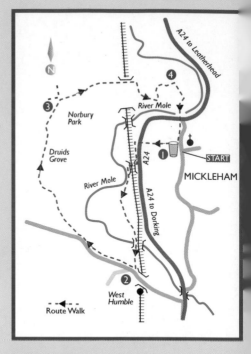

The Walk

① Walk along the small lane at the side of the Running Horses and soon pass through fields to reach the A24. Take care here and cross to the lane opposite and follow it as it swings to the left. At a fork keep left and soon pass under a railway bridge. When the lane divides by a barn go left along a farm track and when this ends continue ahead through a kissing gate. Cross a field towards a second kissing gate to soon meet the river Mole. Cross a footbridge and press

PLACE OF INTEREST NEARBY

The Fire and Iron Gallery at Rowhurst Forge, Oxshott Road, Leatherhead, is known worldwide. Here you can see and buy the most extraordinary range of metalwork from the most delicate jewellery to life-size steel animals. Telephone: 01372 386453.

A wood sculpture in Norbury Park.

woodland and in about ¾ mile look out for a viewpoint sign to your right. Here you will find a couple of welcome seats that make the effort of climbing to this elevated spot all the more worthwhile.

③ Return to the tarmac drive and continue through the woodland a little further to meet a junction of tracks by a sawmill. Go right here and soon pass the entrance to Norbury Park House. This magnificent house was built in 1774 and was once owned by Dr Marie Stopes, the pioneer of family planning clinics. During the early summer months you may well see spikes of orchids amongst the other wildflowers that grow along the edge of this drive as it continues downhill. Eventually the drive zig-zags down the open hillside to meet a small road.

on along the left-hand field edge to pass through yet another kissing gate to reach a road.

② Turn right here along a small lane to the right of an ornate archway. Keep to this lane as it climbs steadily uphill and passes a couple of well-sited houses. Go right on a tarmac drive signposted to Norbury Park and ignore a bridleway to your right in 10 yards or so. Keep to this drive as it leads you through mixed

④ Turn right here and soon the road crosses the river Mole where you again meet the busy A24. Cross to Old London Road opposite and within a short distance you will come to the Running Horses and the end of the stroll.

Lower Kingswood
The Mint Arms

MAP: OS LANDRANGER 187 (GR 248533)	**WALK 12**	**DISTANCE:** $2\frac{1}{4}$ MILES

DIRECTIONS TO START: LOWER KINGSWOOD IS ON THE A217 A MILE NORTH OF JUNCTION 8 OF THE M25. THE MINT ARMS IS IN BUCKLAND ROAD TO YOUR LEFT WHEN COMING FROM THE M25. **PARKING:** IN THE PUB CAR PARK OR ALONG THE ROAD.

This attractive stroll takes you along the edge of Margery Wood where the woodland floor is carpeted by bluebells during spring and the trees resound with birdsong. The route soon turns southwards and crosses the M25 to bring you to the grass covered hilltop of Colley Hill, one of Surrey's prettiest but less well-known beauty spots where you will witness stunning panoramic views across the Surrey countryside. In the distance beyond Reigate, aeroplanes can be seen taking off and landing at Gatwick airport while to the south-west is Leith Hill with Hindhead in the far distance. The short grasses of the chalky soil here are interwoven with many wildflowers that include thyme and speedwell while on the breeze during spring is the scent of hawthorn which makes this a most pleasurable place to pause awhile. The return route passes through the splendours of Margery Wood where elegant beech trees offer fine shade during the heat of summer.

The Mint Arms

I have never been able to work out why Lower Kingswood is so named as it sits 150 feet above Kingswood itself. Perched on top of the breezy North Downs, this small and once fairly isolated community now forms a part of the ever spreading commuterdom that the nearby main road and motorway brings. The original Mint Arms was built 200 years ago and was named after the fields of the herb that once grew in the area. The present building was erected around 1920 and has since been extended and improved and offers a very fine welcome to all that visit.

This traditional pub has a good choice of draught beers that include Flowers IPA, London Pride, Hogs Back TEA, Wadworth 6X, Abbot Ale and Boddingtons Cream as well as Guinness, Stella Artois, Foster's and a wide selection of wines. There is a varied choice from the menu and the blackboard 'specials' in the dining area where I can heartily recommend the lovely home-made pies and puddings. All meals are cooked to order and on Sundays (weekend booking essential) you will not be disappointed by the traditional roast. Food times are 11 am to 2.30 pm and 6 pm to 9.30 pm, Monday to Friday, 11 am to 3 pm and 6 pm to 10 pm on Saturday, and 12 noon to 8 pm on Sunday. During the summer months children can play in the well-designed play area beside the pretty garden and, weather permitting, bar staff attend to a sumptuous barbecue. Telephone: 01737 242957 or 01737 244925.

The Walk

① With your back to the pub go left along the lane and soon pass Dent's Grove and the entrance to Dent's Farm. Just before you reach a National Trust car park, ignore a footpath on your right, but go right on a bridleway that runs along the edge of wonderful woodland. When a small lane is met continue ahead along the bridleway.

② At another lane turn left along it and soon cross the noisy M25 that has, unfortunately, left an indelible scar on this wonderful place. Ignore side turnings to left and right and press on along the lane to pass a coal duty post. These posts marked the boundary where duty was levied on coal entering London; this was originally imposed to aid the rebuilding of London after the Great Fire in 1666 but lapsed in 1889.

③ By a second duty post turn left onto a bridleway through woodland and at a T-junction with another bridleway go left to soon pass through a gate. The way forks here and you should go rightwards to meet the splendours of Colley Hill. This is one of Surrey's prettiest beauty spots and fortunately far less trampled than its much better known counterpart Box Hill, 4 miles west along the downs. The route is ahead along the grassy top of the slope but take your time here as there is so much to see from these heady heights.

PLACE OF INTEREST NEARBY

Just off the A25 at Reigate Heath stands an **unusual old windmill**. Built in 1765 it was later converted to a church in 1862. The roundhouse can seat about fifty and evensong is held once a month from May to October. Open during daylight hours all year.

The view from Colley Hill.

It's a marvellous place to sit and lose oneself in thought.

④ When opposite the castellated water tower, go through a gate to the left of it and re-cross the M25. Here we enter Margery Wood where the shade of the spreading beech trees is welcome on a hot summer's afternoon. Press on along the well-trodden path to reach the National Trust car park where you go through the height barrier and retrace your footsteps along the unmade track to reach the Mint Arms and the end of the walk.

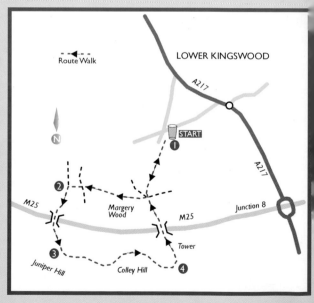

Godstone
The White Hart

MAP: OS LANDRANGER 187 (GR 351515) | **WALK 13** | **DISTANCE:** 2 MILES

DIRECTIONS TO START: GODSTONE IS JUST SOUTH OF JUNCTION 6 OF THE M25 AND THE WHITE HART OVERLOOKS THE VILLAGE GREEN. **PARKING:** IN THE PUB CAR PARK OR OPPOSITE IN A SMALL CAR PARK.

Godstone retains much of its olde worlde charm despite sitting at the junction of two busy main roads. The large tree-lined green and duck pond in the centre of the village complement the many well-preserved old houses and inns in the area. Our route starts by crossing this green before swinging south and then east to pass Leigh Place where a watermill once owned by the Evelyn family manufactured gunpowder for the crown. Later, Charles 1 awarded the contract to the Chilworth gunpowder mills and Leigh Mill reverted back to the more peaceful art of milling grain. To create the constant and steady flow of water these mills required, local streams were dammed to form ponds. As the route swings around to complete the circle we pass one of these pretty ponds to reach a wonderful group of almshouses designed by Sir George Gilbert Scott in the 19th century. Soon a second and larger pond – now a nature reserve – is passed on our return route.

The White Hart

This striking old coaching inn is said by some to originate from the 15th century and takes its name from the badge of King Richard II although no internal evidence of its antiquity has been found to date earlier than the mid-16th century which actually makes it Elizabethan. Never mind, the abundance of genuine old beams and massive doors add atmosphere to the structure that has not much changed since William Cobbett visited and feasted on bread and cheese here on one of his 'rural rides'.

Rather more is on offer today in this large and comfortable pub as the extensive menu reveals. As well as a good choice of starters and puddings, main courses range from steak and kidney pie with chips to duck in plum sauce with all the trimmings. There are always vegetarian options and a children's menu is available. The bar is just bristling with pumps that offer thirst-quenchers such as Pedigree, Wadworth 6X and Boddingtons bitters, Stella Artois and Heineken lagers and Scrumpy Jack and Strongbow ciders. Owned by Whitbread, this large and very pleasant pub and eatery is open from 12 noon to 11 pm on Monday to Saturday and to 10.30 pm on Sundays. Booking for the restaurant is essential. Telephone: 01883 742521.

The Walk

① Cross the road outside the White Hart and go to the left of the village pond. Pass a lovely group of old cottages and continue along a tarmac path to reach a lane. Turn left along the lane and press on where in a dip you will see the footings to Ivy Mill. A watermill has been sited here since Domesday and these remains are the last of a long succession of mills which last worked in 1922. Almost opposite here is a difficult to spot footpath sign where you should turn left, initially along the drive of a bungalow named The Barn.

② Keep ahead along a path that follows field edges to reach a road where you turn left and soon turn right into a short lane. At a road junction cross into Bullbeggars Lane opposite and in 80 yards cross a stile on your right to meet a second in 10 yards. Cross this and continue along the right-hand field edge to pass over the crest of

PLACE OF INTEREST NEARBY

Godstone Farm is a children's farm where they are encouraged to stroke and feed the animals. Just to the south of the village in Tilburstow Hill Road it is open daily from 10 am to 6 pm. Telephone: 01883 742546.

Godstone's village pond and green.

the hill to meet a stile in the fence. Go over this and maintain direction to reach steps leading to a road.

③ The route is ahead along the shady lane but take a couple of moments to view the marvellous 15th century Old Pack House, formerly an inn, just a few yards along the lane on your right. Press on along the lane and pass the grounds of Leigh Place. As the drive turns sharply right, go left over a stile and continue along a rising field edge. Before reaching the crest of the hill turn left by a marker post and follow a well-worn path through woodland to reach a lily-covered pond.

④ The path crosses the man-made dam and soon reaches the graveyard of St Nicholas' church where you continue along an avenue of lime trees. Over to your right is a sarsen stone marking the grave of Edmund Seyfang Taylor nicknamed 'Walker Miles', a man who did so much for London rambling clubs at the end of the 19th century and helped popularise country walking. Pass to the left of the church to soon meet a lane alongside the almshouses and chapel designed by Sir George Gilbert Scott. Our way is along the tarmac path opposite and to the right of Church House and soon we pass Bay Pond, again man-made to serve the watermills of the area. Finally we pass the village hall and end our stroll alongside the White Hart.

The Sands
The Barley Mow

DIRECTIONS TO START: THE SANDS IS JUST EAST OF FARNHAM AND IS SIGNPOSTED FROM THE A31 HOG
BACK AND THE B3001 AT WAVERLEY ABBEY. **PARKING:** IN THE PUB CAR PARK OR ALONG THE ROADSIDE

This interesting and varied stroll starts at The Sands, a small scattered heathland village just south of the Hog's Back by Crooksbury Hill. Our route is along quiet lanes and tracks that pass through pleasant stands of pine to reach the edge of Moor Park. Here, if you wish, is an optional detour to the ruins of Waverley Abbey adding ¾ mile to the stroll. Our route continues on a pretty path above the river Wey as it flows through what was once the parkland of Moor Park. It was here that Jonathan Swift, the writer of *Gulliver's Travels*, lived and fell in love with his 'Stella' back in the 1690s. Near the beginning of this path we pass Mother Ludlam's Cave where the benevolent witch once lived and made her potent brews. After passing Moor Park House our route climbs a short hill to reach open countryside from where we make our return journey back to the Barley Mow and the end of our stroll.

The Barley Mow

The Barley Mow is a pleasant little pub offering a warm welcome to all that pass by this way. Built originally as a dwelling house during the early 1830s, its location at the centre of the village made it ideal for conversion into a pub just a few years later, and a pub it has remained ever since.

The cosy bar offers Courage Best, Greene King IPA and Brakspear bitters as well as a good range of pub food. My last visit was quite late in the year and the Christmas Menu was already in full swing and platefuls of roast turkey with bacon roll, stuffing, cranberry sauce, vegetables and gravy were being consumed with great vigour. The menu is ever changing so whenever you call you will find a good selection. During fine weather in the summer months you can relax at a table in the rather pleasant garden and breathe in the fresh air that contains a slight scent of pine from the dense stands of nearby Crooksbury Hill. Traditional pub hours apply here and food is served from 12 noon to 2 pm each lunchtime, also between 6.30 pm and 9.30 each evening except Sunday. Booking is recommended during peak times. Telephone: 01252 782200.

The Walk

① Our route begins in Smugglers Way at the side of the pub where we climb steadily to the top of Crooksbury Hill. After passing the crest of the hill the road ends and you should carry on downhill along a bridleway where you keep ahead to meet a road.

② Turn right along the road and at a bend turn left on a bridleway alongside Waverley Cottage. Press on along the stony track until another road is reached. Turn right along the road to soon meet a road junction with Camp Hill.

If you wish to visit the ruins of Waverley Abbey go left along Waverley Lane and soon turn left into a small parking area by the gates of Waverley Abbey House (unfortunately dogs are not allowed). Pass through a kissing gate and follow a path alongside the abbey stewpond to reach the interesting ruins. To continue the stroll return to the road junction.

③ Our route continues along Camp Hill for a few feet and then left on a footpath along the gravel driveway of a house. Press on alongside a wall and continue on the woodland path with the river Wey to your left. Very shortly you will pass the entrance to Mother Ludlam's Cave, now almost hidden by ivy and in a rather dangerous condition. Continue along this pleasant path until you eventually pass Moor Park House where you continue through its entrance gates to meet Compton Way.

④ Turn right along the road and when

PLACE OF INTEREST NEARBY

Birdworld and Underwater World makes a fascinating and interesting day out for the whole family. Situated 1 mile south of Farnham at Holt Pound on the A325. Open all year – check times. Telephone: 01420 22140. **The Packhouse Antique Centre** in Tongham Road 1 mile north of The Sands is just the place to poke around for the odd bargain. Open from 10.30 am to 5.30 pm 7 days a week (no dogs). Follow the brown tourist signs. Telephone: 01252 781010.

The ruins of 12th-century Waverley Abbey.

near the top of the hill where the road bends right, continue ahead on a well-marked North Downs Way path. At a field cross a stile and press on along the left-hand edge. The hedge along here is mainly cherry plum and during late July and August will be covered in fruit. At the end of the field maintain direction through woodland.

⑤ After going down steps to a wide crossing track you should turn right along it and pass between the rear of gardens to meet a road. Go right and cross Compton Way and soon turn left into Botany Hill. Press on along the road until a bridlepath is reached on your right.

⑥ Follow this sandy path as it winds its way through woodland. At a post inscribed with the number 577, turn left between barriers and within

yards you find yourself on top of the Soldier's Ring – an early man-made earthwork. Continue down the far side and turn right on a small path to reach a marker post inscribed 576. Turn right here and follow this track until it reaches Smuggler's Way where by turning left you soon meet up with the Barley Mow and the end of the stroll.

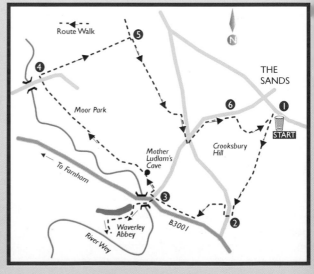

Broadford
The Parrot Inn

| MAP: OS LANDRANGER 186 (GR 997468) | **WALK 15** | DISTANCE: 2¾ MILES |

DIRECTIONS TO START: BROADFORD IS ON THE A248 JUST SOUTH OF SHALFORD. **PARKING:** IN THE PUB CAR PARK OR ALONG THE SMALL ROAD FACING THE PUB.

Broadford is one of those places you have probably passed through without even realising. It's a quiet little settlement nowadays but in the heyday of water transport it formed an important junction of canals for just behind the Parrot pub is Stonebridge Wharf where the warehouses and loading facilities dealt with the movement of wool, grain, timber and coal. Another cargo shipped from here for the slow journey to London was gunpowder from the nearby Chilworth mills.

Starting from this interesting little place we cross the common to reach Shalford and pass by the lovely tile-hung watermill that is now looked after so ably by the National Trust. After going along a quiet residential road we reach the waters of the Wey Navigation near Guildford. The return route follows the scenic canal towpath where gaily painted narrow boats navigate the cool waters during summer and pass through a lock in the water meadows along our route.

The Parrot Inn

The Parrot Inn stands alongside Shalford Common and only a few yards away from the Wey Navigation. Although the old wharf has closed down, many people still visit this charming little place drawn as much by the good food and ales served at the Parrot as by the picturesque waterway.

From the pumps come Courage Best, Brakspear, Ruddles and Wadworth 6X beers, Foster's lagers and to round-off the choice comes Scrumpy Jack cider.

On warm summer days you may choose to sun yourself at a table in the pleasant garden or on the lawn at the front of the pub. For those seeking more comfortable surroundings the pub does have a restaurant area, but wherever you choose to sit, the food is quite splendid and I found it quite hard to choose between the ploughman's lunch and the fine selection of sandwiches, one of which was stuffed with a mozzarella, avocado and tomato filling. For something more substantial take a look at the à la carte menu where you will find a wide choice of dishes that include fried scampi, home-made lasagne served with garlic bread, and steak, Guinness and mushroom pie with all the trimmings. Sunday roasts are always very popular here so it is best to book in advance. Food times are 12 noon to 2.30 pm and 6 pm to 9.30 pm on weekdays and 12 noon to 10 pm at weekends. Telephone: 01483 561400.

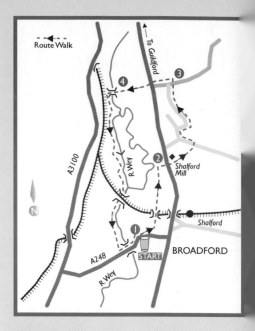

The Walk

① Cross the A248 and go along a footpath over the common signposted to Shalford. Press on ahead alongside a row of cottages and at a fork in the rough track keep left and now follow a footpath signposted to Guildford. Cross a railway bridge and keep ahead on a wide path.

② Eventually at a junction of paths, ignore the path signposted to Guildford and turn right through posts to reach a busy road. Go right along the road and

PLACE OF INTEREST NEARBY

Guildford Boat House in Millbrook is just a few minutes walk from Guildford High Street and offers row boats and canoes for hire in the summer months. Telephone: 01483 504494. The route passes **Shalford Mill** which retains most of its original machinery including the waterwheel. Open daily between 9.30 am and 5 pm. Telephone: 01483 561617.

Shalford watermill.

very pleasant residential road and ignore a cul-de-sac on your left.

③ At a T-junction turn left along the road and at a second T-junction go ahead over the road and a large area of grass to meet a path that leads you through trees to the river Wey.

④ Turn left along the bank of the river for a few yards before crossing a bridge where you should now continue left along the river under eroded sand cliffs. Press on along the bank of the river where, on a bend, you pass a vertical roller that once enabled the horse-drawn barges to negotiate the tight angle. Soon the river goes away to the left and we continue ahead along the towpath of the canalised section to pass lock gates. Press on here and continue under a railway bridge where the designer gave no thought to the beautiful setting. Before long a road is met where you should turn left and cross a road bridge to reach the Parrot Inn within a few yards.

very soon turn left on a lane signed to Shalford Mill. Pass this pretty place and continue ahead over a field to reach a lane. Turn left along the lane and soon turn right into Tilehouse Road. Keep on this

Chilworth
The Percy Arms

| MAP: OS LANDRANGER 186 (GR 030473) | **WALK 16** | DISTANCE: 2¼ MILES |

DIRECTIONS TO START: CHILWORTH IS ON THE A248 HALFWAY BETWEEN SHALFORD AND ALBURY.
PARKING: IN THE PUB CAR PARK OR ALONG THE A248.

This lovely stroll is through a part of the Tillingbourne Valley that William Cobbett described as containing 'two of the most damnable inventions that ever sprang from the minds of men under the influence of the devil! Namely the making of gunpowder and banknotes'. That was in 1822 and oh how things have changed today! A peaceful woodland path takes you past the ruins of the mills that once made their 'damnable' products. After a serious fire the paper mill moved from these rustic surroundings but the gunpowder mills survived here until as late as 1920, although not without incident. During the life of the mills several explosions took place, the most serious in 1901 when six men lost their lives. The leats that drove the mills now ripple through peaceful woodland and picnic tables are placed in a sunlit clearing. The return route is along a hillside path which passes through the grounds of Chilworth Manor, built in the 17th century for one of the original mill owners.

The Percy Arms

The present Percy Arms was built in the early 1920s on the site of a previous pub and takes its name from the Percy family who inherited the Albury Estate which owns much of the area. Since 1990 it has been in the hands of the Greene King brewery and so it will come as no surprise to you that their IPA and Abbot ales flow from the pumps as well as a selection of seasonal ales. A very full menu is available throughout the week which should cover most tastes with children's portions available.

Being not far from the North Downs Way long distance footpath this very friendly pub offers a warm welcome to walkers. One of life's pleasures after a good stroll on a winter's day is being warmed by the roaring log fire and choosing anything from a 'Cajun Chicken and Mulled Plum Chutney Sandwich' to braised lamb with all the trimmings from the menu while supping a fine ale from the pumps. Of course you may visit during summer instead and sit at a table in the large garden that has magnificent views across the meadows to St Martha's church high on its wooded hilltop. Food times are 12 noon to 2 pm and 6 pm to 9.30 pm Monday to Saturday, and from 12 noon to 2.30 pm and 7 pm to 9 pm on Sunday. Unusually the pub has a skittle alley and a petanque terrain – no I hadn't heard of it either! Apparently it is the French game similar to our bowls but often played on rough ground and sometimes called boules. Although booking is not essential here it is advisable on busy weekends. Telephone: 01483 561765.

The Walk

① Leave the Percy Arms and turn left along the A248 where you soon pass the Chilworth Station sign and, a short time later, the village pond. After $1/4$ mile go left on a farm track signposted 'Downs Link' and pass stables. Ahead on the hilltop you will notice St Martha's church some 420 feet above you. Just after the track crosses a stream, go left on a path through woodland and pass an information board explaining the gunpowder making process. Press on along this now peaceful path and pass the more recent workings and ignore any side paths. Gunpowder was made here from the 16th century and among the trees and undergrowth you will detect the remains of these early gunpowder mills. Some of the leats that powered them still flow through the woodland and children often play in the cool shallow water. In a clearing are picnic tables and standing proudly on display are the millstones that were once so central to the industry

② The path ends by a small gatehouse and iron gateway that formed the entrance to the workings that at one stage employed around 400 workers. Turn right here and continue along the road and pass a small lake where the leats rejoin the Tilling Bourne before it splashes through an arch below us. Go right into Halfpenny Lane, a name that indicates the price of the toll paid per load once carried along

PLACE OF INTEREST NEARBY

Chilworth Manor was rebuilt for Vincent Randyll, a gunpowder mill owner in the 17th century and is open to the public on Wednesday to Sunday between April and August from 2 pm to 6 pm.

Millstones lining the path through the woodland.

here. When the road bends to the left continue ahead along the driveway to Chilworth Manor.

③ Walk along this enjoyable drive and with Chilworth Manor in sight over a stone wall, look out for a broad bridleway on your right which you should now take. Soon ignore a footpath to your left and press on ahead. The path narrows and continues gently downhill where it gives views over the woodland you passed through earlier. When it reaches a farm track press on ahead.

④ Soon you will recognise the track previously walked where you should now keep ahead to pass the stables and reach the A248. Turn right and retrace your steps back to the Percy Arms and the end of this very pleasant stroll.

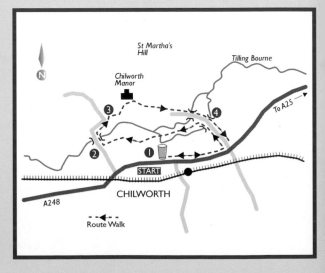

Shere
The Prince of Wales

| MAP: OS LANDRANGER 187 (GR 073477) | **WALK 17** | DISTANCE: 2¼ MILES |

DIRECTIONS TO START: SHERE IS 1 MILE WEST OF GOMSHALL AND IS SIGNPOSTED FROM THE A25. CROSS THE TILLING BOURNE IN THE CENTRE OF THE VILLAGE AND AHEAD WILL BE SEEN THE PRINCE OF WALES.
PARKING: IN THE PUB CAR PARK OR AROUND THE VILLAGE.

Writers on Surrey often describe Shere as the jewel in the county's crown and I am not about to argue with that. Narrow streets, timbered houses, the 12th century St James's church and a tiny triangular green all blend to create a wonderful setting. But that is not all, for flowing through the village centre are the shimmering waters of the Tilling Bourne, once the power source for dozens of mills.

The circuit starts by passing the old church before following a rising path across fields where you will see unspoiled pastoral views over Shere. The return route passes through tranquil woodland before we meet an enjoyable downhill grassy track along an avenue of gnarled chestnut trees. With magnificent views over the valley we soon find ourselves alongside the Tilling Bourne where we follow its course back to the village and pass some delightful cottages along the way.

The Prince of Wales

Everyone finds a warm and friendly welcome in this superb freehouse that sits in Shere Lane almost at the centre of the village. Built around 1890, the pub is sited in what was once a hop field and is one of the newer buildings in this old rose-adorned community.

A good range of sandwiches, baps, ploughman's and jacket potato selections are on offer as well as meals such as grilled fresh salmon fillet or Cajun chicken. When I last visited I treated myself to 'Cod O' Crikey' which is described in the menu as 'the biggest fish you ever did see'. Served with a wedge of lemon with salad and fries it really did live up to its name. Children are most welcome and have their own menu and vegetarians will always find a mouth-watering meal. On Sundays (booking essential) comes the traditional roast dinner with either pork, beef or lamb accompanied by a fair lashing of roast potatoes and vegetables. No matter when you visit always look out for the 'specials' written up on the blackboards. Food times are 12 noon to 2.30 pm and 6 pm to 9 pm Monday to Saturday, and 12 noon to 2.30 pm on Sunday. From the pumps come Foster's and Stella lagers plus Beamish Red, Brakspear and Flowers bitters while wine is available by the glass or bottle. Telephone: 01483 202313.

The Walk

① From the Prince of Wales walk downhill to soon meet the tiny triangular green where you should turn right. When almost past St James's church take a small gated path on your right. Go through a second gate and press on ahead across a field. Maintain direction through another gate and soon cross a railway bridge where you press on over another field.

② At the end of this field turn right on a bridleway alongside the wall of a house. Soon the bridleway goes between gardens to reach a road. Turn right along the road for 40 yards and then turn left on a footpath. Keep to this path as it swings rightwards and skirts a large garden before becoming enclosed between fences.

③ When a road is met continue on the path opposite and follow it through mixed woodland that offers cool dappled shade on warm days. Soon a small lane is met where you go right and pass three houses to meet a railway crossing gate. Go through this gate but don't forget to stop, look and listen before crossing the railway line. At the other side ignore a path to your right and continue ahead through more woodland to reach a road junction.

④ Maintain direction along the road ahead signposted to Albury. Soon at a bend by a house called South Lodge go right on the centre of three paths and continue downhill between fields

PLACE OF INTEREST NEARBY

The Silent Pool, located 1 mile west of Shere on the A25 has become a part of local folklore due to the writings of the Victorian writer Martin Tupper. The clear waters of the chalk spring are visited by people who enjoy the tranquillity of the pool.

A pretty Shere cottage built in 1705.

following an avenue of old chestnut trees.

⑤ At the end of the field go through a gate to meet the Tilling Bourne by a ford. Turn right here through a kissing gate and continue on a field path with the stream to your left. Pass through a second kissing gate and bear left along a wide track. Keep ahead now and pass pretty cottages to soon reach the centre of the village where you should now turn right for the Prince of Wales and the end of the stroll.

57

Friday Street
The Stephan Langton Inn

| MAP: OS LANDRANGER 187 (GR 127455) | WALK 18 | DISTANCE: $1^3/_4$ OR $3^3/_4$ MILES |

DIRECTIONS TO START: TURN OFF THE A25 ABOUT 2 MILES WEST OF DORKING AND FOLLOW SIGNS TO FRIDAY STREET. **PARKING:** NO PARKING IN FRIDAY STREET AND VERY LIMITED BY THE STEPHAN LANGTON INN SO PARK IN THE ABINGER COMMON FREE CAR PARK JUST OUTSIDE THE HAMLET (GR 126458).

This enchanting stroll is through the splendid woodland that covers the northern slopes of Leith Hill and offers fine shade from the sun on hot days. The route is moderately easy for this part of the Surrey Hills and no hill is too strenuous to scale but the longer stroll contains one quite steep descent.

We leave Friday Street by following a small brook through trees to reach Abinger Bottom where we turn westwards to reach St James's Well on the south-eastern edge of Abinger Common village. The shorter route returns to Friday Street from here while the longer one continues over the wooded common and heads north to St James's church and the Abinger Hatch pub. The village green here retains its old stocks, roaming geese and rural charm. Leaving this quiet scene behind we continue through more woodland to reach the end of our stroll.

The Stephan Langton

The Stephan Langton Inn and Restaurant is the full name of this fine establishment, and for the second time in this little book Stephan Langton gets a mention (see Stroll 1). However, the only link with him and Friday Street is through a fictitious and rather fanciful story written in 1858 by the local poet Martin Tupper who also managed to slip 'The Silent Pool' near Shere and 'The Baron's Cave' in Reigate into legend.

Many a time I have sat on the pleasant patio here after a stroll and enjoyed a filling ploughman's lunch washed down by a glass of good ale from the pumps that dispense Harveys Sussex, London Pride, Young's Special and Bass bitters. If you fancy something slightly more refined then I highly recommend you sample one of the exquisite meals from the à la carte menu in the restaurant where you will find a choice of 17 different wines to accompany your meal. Somewhere in-between the two is the ever changing 'specials' menu as well as one for children and a selection of mouth-watering vegetarian food. Meal times are 12.30 pm to 3 pm and 7 pm to 10 pm Tuesday to Saturday, and from 12.30 pm to 4 pm on Sunday. Booking is essential in the very popular restaurant on Thursday, Friday and Saturday evenings. Telephone: 01306 730775.

The Walk

① From the Abinger Common car park walk down the road to meet the hammer pond at Friday Street. Turn right here along a narrow lane to come upon the Stephan Langton Inn. The route passes the pub and very soon, when the lane ends abruptly, press on ahead along an uphill track beside a small brook.

② The path ends at a lane and you should turn right along it. After going around a left bend, look out for a crossing path by wooden railings. Stay on the lane for a further 20 yards and branch off to the right along a bridleway. Keep ahead over a crossing path and again at a fork by a large pine tree to reach a country lane.

③ To your left is St James's Well built in 1895 by a descendant of the famous diarist, John Evelyn. For the shorter stroll turn right along the lane and in 100 yards turn right again into a narrow road that leads you to the car park. The longer stroll continues ahead alongside the green and forward on a path beside Pasturewood Cottage. Go over a crossing track and up a small gully. At a forestry track maintain direction and when this track turns sharply right, again keep ahead. The path narrows and goes steeply downhill to meet a stile.

④ Cross this stile and another to your right and press on along a very pleasant

PLACE OF INTEREST NEARBY

Leith Hill Tower, south of Friday Street, was built in 1766 by the eccentric Richard Hull. He is buried upside down beneath it in his belief that the world would turn on its axis and he 'wished to stand before his Maker right way up'. Open from April to September on Wednesdays and weekends from 2 pm to 5 pm.

The picturesque hammer pond at Friday Street.

the graveyard in garden lies Norman mott and a littl further away an out of sight something muc older, th remains of Mesolithic pi dwelling from 4,000 years ag making this one of the oldes villages in England. The route continues along a lane to

grassy track. During summer the honeysuckle that adorns the birch trees along here sends out its scent which is then suspended on the warm breeze. When this track turns sharply right proceed ahead along a well-worn path. At a fork in the path under power cables keep left and press on between holly bushes to meet a stile at a field edge.

⑤ Go over the stile and the field ahead to another stile on the far side. Cross this and go down steps to meet a lane. Go forward and breathe in the enchantment of the village green where ducks and geese are free to wander. Ahead is St James's church with its mellow stone now much restored due to a hit by a doodlebug in the Second World War. Through

the right of the Abinger Hatch pub. At a T-junction turn right and after 150 yards bear left along a bridleway that brings you to the road where you maintain direction ahead to reach the Abinger Common car park and the end of the stroll.

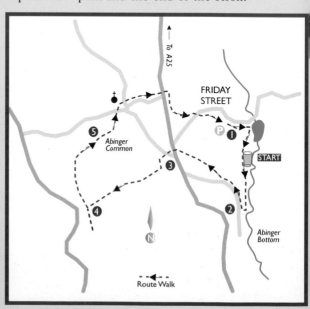

Brockham
The Royal Oak

MAP: OS LANDRANGER 187 (GR 198496) **WALK 19** **DISTANCE:** $2^3/_4$ MILES

DIRECTIONS TO START: BROCKHAM IS 1 MILE SOUTH OF THE A25 ALMOST HALFWAY BETWEEN REIGATE AND DORKING. **PARKING:** IN THE PUB CAR PARK OR AROUND THE VILLAGE GREEN.

Nestling under the slopes of Box Hill is the delightful village of Brockham, known far and wide for its charming green and old village pump. Surrounding this pleasing scene are pretty houses of all ages resplendent with roses. The village green hosts one of Surrey's largest bonfires on Guy Fawkes night and draws onlookers from miles around, but fortunately it soon recovers its dignified posture.

This lovely pastoral stroll crosses Tanner's Brook to join a level wildflower and tree lined bridleway that takes you over Betchworth Park golf course. The turning point comes as we pass the clubhouse and then follow paths through a patchwork of open fields where there are pretty views across the countryside to the rising slopes of Box Hill. The stroll is suitable for any time of the year but it is unsurpassed during spring when the wayside flowers are in bloom.

The Royal Oak

The Royal Oak is one of those pubs that on a lovely summer's day you may well find hard to leave. Many a time I have sat at a table in the shade of a gaily coloured umbrella and lunched on a fine Cheddar ploughman's washed down with a pint of real ale. To the rear there is an area set aside for children so that they can burn off the extra energy they always seem to have while you relax in the pretty garden. Owned by Punch Taverns, the 150 year old pub – quite young really for a Surrey village pub – has the slopes of Box Hill as a backdrop while the frontage faces the village green which still retains its much photographed water pump.

A good selection of food, including children's portions, is offered from the ever changing menu and the 'daily specials' blackboards which cover all tastes including vegetarian. Food times are 12 noon to 2 pm and 6.30 pm to 9.30 pm on Monday to Saturday, and all day on Sunday from 12 noon to 10.30 pm. From the pumps come Harveys, Broadside, Wadworth 6X and London Pride bitters plus Carlsberg lager. During the colder winter months the comfortable bar is heated by a roaring log fire which creates a cosy atmosphere which you will find even harder to leave. This is a popular little pub and you will need to book a table if you want a sit down meal here. Telephone: 01737 843241.

The Walk

① From the Royal Oak cross the green to the village pump and continue along Old School Lane ahead where you soon cro[ss] Tanner's Brook and turn right along [a] bridleway. After passing a couple of house[s] this pleasant level track passes betwee[n] fields and is bordered by clouds o[f] flowering cow parsley during springtim[e.] Press on along this lovely track as [it] becomes tree lined and goes betwee[n] the fairways of Betchworth Park Go[lf] Club.

② When eventually the track comes to [a] driveway, cross to the footpath opposit[e] and pass alongside the golfers' car park. A[t] the end of the car park turn left on [a] footpath that leads you past the front o[f] the clubhouse and between a bungalo[w] and some sheds. Continue ahead throug[h] trees and pass a chestnut tree with a hug[e] girth. As you come out of the trees g[o] ahead to a stile on the opposite side of [a] fairway, being careful to watch out fo[r] flying golf balls coming from your right. Cross the field ahead to another stile an[d] go over a railway bridge. Press on ahead t[o] a third stile which you also cross.

③ Turn left along a farm track and now g[o] under a railway bridge. Keep ahead here on a farm track between fields. There are magnificent views across the fields to Box Hill from this track and additionally, if you are lucky as I was when last passing this way, you may catch a glimpse of one or two

PLACE OF INTEREST NEARBY

Denbies Wine Estate in London Road, (A24) Dorking is the largest vineyard in Britain. There are tours and tastings between 11 am and 4 pm Monday to Saturday and between 12 noon and 4 pm on Sunday. Enjoy a light lunch or browse in the wine shop. Open all year round. Telephone: 01306 876616.

The well at Brockham.

deer grazing. At a fingerpost go right for a couple of yards or so and then left to cross a stile and follow the left-hand edge of the field ahead, still maintaining your original direction. At the end of this field press on to reach a stile by a brook.

④ Cross the stile and turn immediately left and pass the buildings of Pondtail Farm. Continue over the farm lane and maintain direction. Finally, cross a stile to meet the bridleway we passed along earlier where you should now turn right to reach Old School Lane. At the

road bear left to reach Brockham village green, the Royal Oak and the end of the walk.

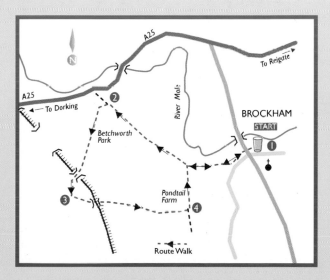

Leigh
The Plough

DIRECTIONS TO START: LEIGH IS 3 MILES SOUTH OF THE A25 AT BETCHWORTH. PASS THROUGH BETCHWORTH VILLAGE AND FOLLOW SIGNS TO LEIGH. **PARKING:** IN THE PUB CAR PARK OR BY THE VILLAGE GREEN.

There are two things you should know about Leigh, the first is that it is pronounced 'Lye' and the second that it is the epitome of an old English village. Set in the Weald near Gatwick airport, Leigh has a traditional village green where a wooden structure now protects the old village pump while behind is the Victorian school building. The lovely green is bordered by the 15th century Priests' House to the east and St Bartholomew's church to the north while on the western boundary is the weather-boarded Plough. The church and the pub also date back to the 15th century although very little of the original fabric exists today.

This short stroll is over level fields with extensive views where we discover a tributary of the river Mole. Leigh was one of Surrey's 'iron villages' and this small stream once provided the power for the village furnace. More scenic fields follow as our circular route again crosses the stream and soon ends back at the village green.

The Plough

Parts of this lovely old village pub date back to the 15th century when it was a coaching inn so it must have seen an awful lot of changes in village life. It was a lovely summer's day when I visited and being early I was able to sit at a table in the charming garden that is surrounded by a wooden trellis adorned by beautiful rambling roses. As you would expect there are exposed beams in the bar but unfortunately no open fire to sit around after a stroll on a cold frosty morning, but don't let that put you off as the place just oozes atmosphere and warmth.

For the ale enthusiast the pumps deliver Sussex, Broadwood, Festive and Old Ale bitters plus an additional seasonal real ale every month. As you would expect from a King & Barnes owned pub there is an excellent choice of food ranging from simple bar snacks to an à la carte menu, all with children sized portions and a vegetarian selection. Food is served from 12 noon to 2 pm and 7 pm to 10 pm on Monday to Saturday and from 12 noon to 10 pm on Sundays. This is a very popular pub on a summers' day which makes booking for a sit down meal essential. Telephone: 01306 611348.

The Walk

① From the Plough turn left and walk along a lane where you soon pass St Bartholomew's church. Within yards go right through a kissing gate at a bend and go diagonally left ahead on a well-trodden path over a field. Aim for a house in the

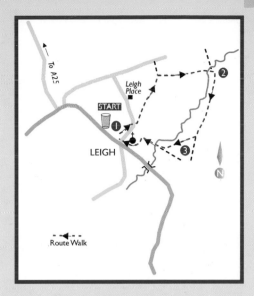

distance and when the far corner of the field is reached keep ahead on the left-hand field edge with a ditch to your left. Ignore a stile on your left and press on ahead. A couple of more fields follow where you maintain direction to reach a wooden bridge that crosses a tributary of the river Mole.

② Go over the bridge and a stile immediately ahead of you. Now swing diagonally right and cross two further stiles to reach a large field. Follow the right-hand edge of the field but as the field edge swings away to your right maintain direction across the field and aim for a stile in a hawthorn hedge ahead of you.

PLACE OF INTEREST NEARBY

Gatwick Zoo and Aviaries, to the south of Leigh, near Charlwood, is a children's zoo containing small monkeys, wallabies, emus, otters, meerkats and a host of butterflies. Open all year from 10.30 am to 6 pm or dusk during winter. Telephone: 01293 862312.

One of the attractive cottages near the village green.

③ Cross this and follow the right-hand field edge to reach a stile beside a gate. Cross this and go diagonally half right across a field keeping a wire fence close to your right. At the far side of this field cross a stile and turn right. Soon re-cross the stream and a field to reach an enclosed path that leads you to the graveyard of St Bartholomew's church. Keep to the left of the church and when the path turns right to a lychgate press on ahead to go through a wooden gate to reach the wonderful village green and the end of the stroll.

Outwood
The Bell

MAP: OS LANDRANGER 187 (GR 327456)   **WALK 21**   **DISTANCE:** 4 MILES

DIRECTIONS TO START: GO SOUTH FROM THE A25 AT BLETCHINGLEY ON OUTWOOD LANE FOR 3 MILES TO REACH OUTWOOD COMMON. **PARKING:** IN THE PUB CAR PARK OR IN THE NATIONAL TRUST CAR PARK ON THE COMMON.

The small hamlet of Outwood sits on an outcrop of sandstone surrounded by Wealden clay and is far enough away from a railway to have been saved from the ravages of Victorian commuterdom. Much of this lovely, and still quite remote, area has been preserved by the generosity of the Lloyd family who 50 years ago donated 2,500 acres of the Harewood Estate to the National Trust. Our stroll starts on Outwood Common which is dominated by a gloriously preserved windmill built way back in 1665. This splendid post mill is England's oldest working mill and if the wind is right on Sundays during summer the sails will be seen sweeping the sky. Our route takes us through a patchwork of fields and beside hedgerows brimming with wildflowers and small birds during summer. This is a lovely circuit at any time of year and you will enjoy the panoramic views across the adjoining countryside.

The Bell

Dating from the 17th century, the mellow half tile-hung frontage of this lovely old coaching inn disguises its age well behind a good coverage of spreading ivy. One oddity on display here on the front wall is a quarter-ton bell that comes from the ruins of a local monastery. The cosy bar, which is said to be haunted, is decorated in a highwayman theme and is warmed by a roaring open fire during the cold winter months.

Sink into the quiet country atmosphere here and allow yourself to be tempted by the huge selection of food that is on offer from 12 noon until 9.30 pm each day (there is a break between 2 pm and 6.30 pm on Saturdays). I tucked into a large mushroom risotto from the Country Garden menu while lashings of home-made game pie from the Fresh from the Farm menu were being consumed at the next table. Booking is essential at weekends and bank holidays if you are not to be disappointed. From the pumps come Harveys Best and Young's Bitter plus an interesting and ever changing selection of guest ales. There is a pretty garden where you may relax in the summer sun after a good country stroll. Telephone: 01342 842989.

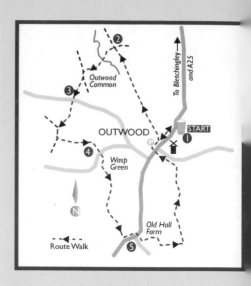

left to meet this lane. At a fork keep left and soon as it abruptly ends, go ahead and cross a stile. Keep ahead through a meadow to reach a field by a post. Press on along the edge of this long sloping field to cross a stile by an oak tree.

② Turn left at this stile and continue along the left edge of a field. Cross a stream to meet a stile ahead. Cross this and keep ahead alongside a hedge decorated with wild roses in summer. Cross a stile in the far corner of the field to meet a bridleway where you now turn left and enter woodland. After 130 yards go right on a narrower path under power cables and pass a peaceful woodland pool. Ignore side paths and keep ahead to soon reach a road.

The Walk

① From the Bell turn left towards the windmill and then right on a signposted path along a narrow lane passing Windmill Garage. If you have parked in the National Trust car park go back to the road and turn

PLACE OF INTEREST NEARBY
Outwood Post Mill is open to the public on Sundays and bank holidays from Easter to the end of October between the hours of 2 pm and 6 pm. Telephone: 01342 843458.

Outwood Mill.

③ Cross to the footpath opposite and soon continue along a field edge. Cross a stile to your left 30 yards before the end of the field. Now follow the right-hand edge of this field to meet two stiles. Go over the left-hand stile and maintain direction through a meadow. Cross a stile by a field gate and continue ahead between farm buildings to reach a lane.

④ Turn right along the lane to meet a road junction where you keep ahead on a signposted footpath. Soon cross a stile and press on along the right-hand field edge. Cross a second stile and a small brook and turn left. In no more than 60 yards go over the brook and a stile and turn right. Now follow the waymarked signs through a series of fields with breathtaking views across the Weald. Finally the path follows

a small stream through a ribbon of woodland to meet a road.

⑤ Turn left at the road and soon go right into Cogmans Lane. In 10 yards go left to a farm gate where you ignore an obvious stile but seek out a stile hidden to the left of the gate. Press on between farm buildings and along the farm track as it first goes right and then left when confronted by a gate ahead. Eventually it reaches a small driveway where you should turn left along the drive and pass a house. Keep ahead on a pretty byway until you eventually reach a road. Now you are within sight of the windmill and you should turn left along the road to meet up with Outwood Common and the end of the stroll.

Lingfield
The Hare and Hounds

MAP: OS LANDRANGER 187 (GR 388448) **WALK 22** **DISTANCE:** 2¼ MILES

DIRECTIONS TO START: FROM THE A22 SOUTH OF GODSTONE TURN ONTO THE B2029 AT BLINDLEY HEATH AND AFTER 1½ MILES TURN LEFT INTO LINGFIELD COMMON ROAD TO REACH THE PUB AFTER ½ MILE. FROM THE SOUTH FOLLOWING THE B2029 OUT OF LINGFIELD AND TURN RIGHT. **PARKING:** IN THE PUB CAR PARK OR ALONG VERGES.

This enthralling stroll has the perfect mix of village streets and pastoral countryside. Starting at Lingfield Common the route passes over fields with fine views across peaceful rural landscapes. A quiet road brings us to the centre of Lingfield where we meet up with the village cage and St Peter's Cross. The cross was erected in 1473 and the cage was added in 1773. Alongside is a wonderfully-kept pond and flower garden where there are a couple of welcoming seats. Our route continues along the High Street and then through the church close with its well-kept 16th century houses; older still is the church itself and just to the north we pass the timber-framed Old Guest House. This splendid 15th century house has been well restored and is now the home of the public library. After this dusting of history we continue over peaceful meadows and through an area devoted to wildlife to soon return to the pub and the end of our stroll.

The Hare and Hounds

This lovely Victorian pub and eatery is tucked away on the outskirts of Lingfield and is not to be missed. Bar snacks are available and meals are also served in the pretty dining room from 12 noon to 2.30 pm and 6.30 pm to 9.30 pm on weekdays while at weekends (booking essential) food is served all day. Childen's portions are available and there is always a vegetarian selection. If by some strange quirk you are not tempted by the gastronomic delights (which may include some Japanese and Thai dishes) whose aromas waft invitingly from the kitchen then quench your thirst on the good selection of beers that include Greene King, Flowers, Wadworth 6X, Tetley's Smooth, Guinness, Carlsberg Export and Stella lagers. For your further enjoyment, during the summer months there is a well-kept garden for you to relax in. Telephone: 01342 832351.

The Walk

① From the Hare and Hounds go rightwards alongside the road and immediately after passing Providence Cottage turn left into a narrow lane. At a fork in this little lane keep to the right and go ahead on a well-trodden path. Pass through kissing gates to meet a driveway and continue leftwards along it. Cross a stile alongside a bungalow and keep ahead on an enclosed path. Cross another stile and a field to reach a cattle trough with a field gate beyond.

② Turn left just before this gate and keep to the right-hand field edge. Ignore a stile on your right and continue to the top corner of the field. Go over a stile in front of you to maintain direction along an enclosed path. When it meets a wide track press on ahead ignoring a path to your right and before long a road is met.

③ Turn right along this pleasant residential road to reach the busy B2029. Turn left here and almost immediately you will find yourself by St Peter's Cross and the village cage. After exploring this unusual village feature pass the pond and press on along the road to reach a small roundabout. Bear left here and continue along the High Street passing buildings of a more recent age.

④ Eventually turn left into Church Road and within yards of passing the Star Inn bear left into the church close where there are 15th century houses including an earlier Star Inn. Enter the churchyard and pass to the right of the church then continue down steps alongside the Old Guest House on your left to meet the road.

⑤ Go ahead on the path opposite and pass through a kissing gate. Remain in a forward direction over an open grassy area and a couple of meadows to eventually

PLACE OF INTEREST NEARBY

Haxted Mill is a working watermill museum alongside the river Eden 2 miles to the east of the pub. Open from 1pm to 5pm from April to September on Wednesdays, Saturdays, Sundays and bank holidays. Telephone: 01732 862914.

A delightful corner of Lingfield.

pass a house and meet a driveway. Press on ahead along the drive and soon go over a stile on your right. Cross the meadow to another stile. Go over this and turn left on a path to soon reach Lingfield Common Road where, by turning right, you come to the Hare and Hounds and the end of the stroll.

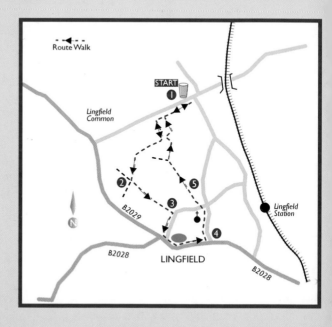

Frensham
The Holly Bush

MAP: OS LANDRANGER 186 (GR 845422) | **WALK 23** | **DISTANCE:** 4 MILES

DIRECTIONS TO START: FRENSHAM SITS ON THE A287 SOME 2½ MILES SOUTH OF FARNHAM. PARKING: IN THE PUB CAR PARK OR BY THE CRICKET PITCH ALONG SHORTFIELD ROAD A FEW YARDS EAST OF THE PUB.

Frensham is known far and wide for its large lakes and its airy open area of heathland that makes up the Country Park. Nestling up against the Hampshire border, this marvellous place is a delight to the visitor. The village itself is rather spread out but the core surrounds St Mary's church where legend has it that the large copper cauldron came from Mother Ludlam's Cave in nearby Moor Park many centuries ago. After passing this interesting little church our way cuts across the common to meet up with Frensham Great Pond where sail boats take advantage of the wide expanse of water. Here we follow the shoreline westwards for a while to reach the shady banks of the river Wey South Branch as it flows through peaceful woodland. By following the course of the river we find ourselves walking along a quiet lane before cutting between fields to find ourselves back at the pub and the end of the stroll.

The Holly Bush

This charming pub sits just down the lane from the picturesque cricket ground and during the summer the cricketers and onlookers alike quench their thirsts here. The welcoming and comfortable bar offers Ruddles Best, Bombardier and Old Speckled Hen bitters from the pumps as well as a pretty good selection of wines. As for the food there is an even bigger choice and I counted four menus just packed with mouth-watering choices from a simple platter of pork sausages, egg and chips to a large grilled steak with all the trimmings. Keep an eye open for the 'specials' blackboard with the chef's daily choice. It is good to see that children are catered for and have their own range of meals and are also able to opt for smaller portions from the main menu. Food is served from 12 noon to 2 pm every day. Outside is a pleasant garden where you can breathe in the country air and where children have their own small play area. Booking a table in advance is necessary if wishing to eat a sit down meal here. Telephone: 01252 793593.

The Walk

① Leave the Holly Bush and walk back towards the A287. Enter the cricket ground and head towards a group of four sweet chestnut trees. If you have parked here then these trees are to the left of the cricket pitch. From these trees bear rightwards around the perimeter of the cricket pitch that has been scooped out of the hillside and soon you will see a stile in the fence ahead of you. Go over this and continue diagonally right down a slope to soon meet a bridge over a brook. Cross the bridge and continue between fields on a sunken path. Just after passing to the right of cottages go left on a narrow footpath, cross a drive and press on ahead downhill to finally meet a T-junction. Turn left here and soon meet a bridge over the river Wey.

② Cross the bridge and press on until the path reaches a road beside St Mary's church. Turn left for a few yards and then turn right into Lovers Lane. At the end continue along a path and at a road keep ahead on the path opposite. At another road turn right along it for ¼ mile and then go left along the drive leading to Frensham Great Pond car park. Pass the information centre to reach the sandy shore.

③ Turn right along the shoreline. Some areas are fenced off so that the plantlife can recover from the pounding of many feet but you will be able to remain quite close to the shore. At a road turn left to

...ensham Great Pond.

...on reach the Frensham Pond Hotel. Pass ...the right of the hotel and turn right on a ...otpath when opposite the car park ...trance.

...) Keep to this path as it passes an idyllic ...nd and soon cross a small weir with ...ution. Now turn left and continue along ...pleasing woodland path with the river ...ey South Branch to your left. At a wider ...ack bear left along it and later ignore a ...idge to your left. Keep ahead to ...entually meet a drive where you pass ...etween wrought iron gates to meet a ...ad.

...) Turn left along the road and very soon ...rn right along a road signposted to ...illbridge. After $^1/_2$ mile turn right into ...ammondswood Road and soon ignore

paths to left and right. Keep ahead along the track to meet a direction post. Bear left here and retrace your steps along the path between fields where you soon cross the small brook. Bear right up the slope to meet up with the stile in the fence of the recreation ground. Press on around the perimeter of the cricket pitch to find yourself back at the Holly Bush and the end of our stroll.

PLACE OF INTEREST NEARBY

Why not explore the pleasures of **Farnham**? West Street is full of Georgian architecture while Castle Street has early 17th century almshouses and, of course, Farnham Castle and Keep at the top, the latter open from 1st April to 1st November from 10 am to 6 pm. Telephone: 01252 713393.

Elstead
The Woolpack

MAP: OS LANDRANGER 186 (GR 908437)   **WALK 24**   **DISTANCE:** $3^3/_4$ MILES

DIRECTIONS TO START: ELSTEAD 2 MILES WEST OF MILFORD ON THE B3001. THE PUB IS BY THE TRIANGULAR VILLAGE GREEN. **PARKING:** IN THE PUB CAR PARK OR AROUND THE VILLAGE.

The oldest part of Elstead is centred on its little green where the blacksmith's forge faces the Woolpack public house. The river Wey passes under a 700 year old bridge on the western edge of the village and beyond that in the water meadows is Elstead Mill. The large mill building became a worsted factory employing around 60 locals but has now been converted to a restaurant.

The stroll soon leaves the village green behind and we pass along a pleasant lane lined by small houses with pretty gardens. As the way swings south it brings us to a lovely track that crosses Royal Common where fine birch and oak trees grow amongst the bracken. Before long the still waters of a peaceful pond are reached where it is worth sitting awhile to take in the beauty. Continuing on, we cross the meadows of Pot Common where during summer you will be accompanied by a host of butterflies feeding on the hedgerow flowers.

The Woolpack

The pub's name recalls the days from the 16th century when the village of Elstead was an important wool centre and the building itself served as a wool store. Eventually, when the local wool trade declined, the enterprising owner converted the lovely tile-hung building into a public house that is now owned by Allied Domecq. Facing the small triangular green, it is at the hub of the village, and like many other village pubs has chosen to ignore the new wave of 'all day' opening establishments and confines itself to traditional opening hours.

The ever changing menu offers a fine selection of good cooked meals, including many pub favourites, that are available from 12 noon to 2 pm and 7 pm to 10.45 pm every day except on Sunday when serving is halted at 9 pm. Beers on draught to quench any thirst before or after your stroll include Greene King Abbot Ale and Fuller's London Pride while a selection of wine is sold by the glass or bottle. There is a pleasant garden to the side of the pub where you can relax on warm days while children enjoy their own play area. Telephone: 01252 703106.

bungalows with pretty gardens and maintain direction at a road junction.

② Finally as the lane turns sharply left and enters a garden keep ahead along a wide grassy track. At a fork bear left on a narrower public footpath. After passing through woodland and between fields the path comes to an open grassy area. Bear left here and follow a cart track to reach a parking area where you continue ahead to meet a road. Turn right along the road and at a T-junction turn left along the B3001.

③ After 200 yards turn right into a small parking area and pass by a barrier. Keep to the tarmac drive as it leads you over Royal Common. Look out for a pretty pond on your right that makes the perfect picnic place. Within yards of passing this

The Walk

① As you come out of the Woolpack turn left through the car park and turn left again along Back Lane to pass the rear of the premises. Before long a road is met where you should turn left again to meet the B3001. Cross the road and continue along Ham Lane opposite. Pass small

Admiring the view at Royal Common.

excellent spot, turn right along a well-trodden path and soon you will meet and pass two idyllic cottages. Press on ahead along a quiet drive between tall pine trees.

④ After passing through gateposts to meet a road you should turn left along a shady bridleway. At a fork in the track keep to the right and as the path narrows ignore a stile beside a field gate. After about 300 yards when alongside an MOD sign, cross a stile to your right by a gate and follow the left-hand field edge.

⑤ A series of fields with lovely open views now follow where you ignore all side paths and remain in a forward direction at all times. Later cross a farm track and continue over a field to finally meet a narrow downhill path that leads you between gardens to reach a road. Turn right here to soon meet up with the Woolpack pub and the end of the stroll.

Compton
The Withies Inn

MAP: OS LANDRANGER 186 (GR 964467)   **WALK 25**   **DISTANCE:** 2¼ MILES

DIRECTIONS TO START: COMPTON IS ½ MILE EAST OF THE A3 AND SITS ON THE B3000 JUST SOUTH OF GUILDFORD. THE WITHIES INN IS IN WITHIES LANE AND IS SIGNED FROM THE B3000. **PARKING:** IN THE PUB CAR PARK OR ALONG VERGES.

There are 25 Comptons in England but the one we are about to explore is possibly the most interesting. This ancient village stands on the Pilgrims' Way below the southern slopes of the Hog's Back and very fortunately for us has long been bypassed by the busy A3. For almost a century the village has drawn visitors from far and wide through its association with G.F. Watts, the Victorian artist. After passing through mature woodland our route brings us to the Watts Gallery, built after his death in 1904 by his wife as a shrine. A short and well worthwhile detour to the nearby graveyard will bring you to the Watts Chapel, a bright red terracotta building in the shape of a Greek cross and decorated internally in a stunning art nouveau style. The route continues along a part of the North Downs Way long distance path before turning south and passing Polsted Manor on our return to Compton.

The Withies Inn

Set well back among the trees along the narrow little lane that is named after it is the wonderful old Withies Inn dating from the 16th century. Enter this fine country pub and experience the warm welcome and friendly atmosphere exuded by the staff. Eat here and enjoy large helpings of sumptuous home-cooked food from the changing menu.

Food is served on Monday to Saturday at lunchtime and in the evenings, but beware if visiting on Sundays as last orders for food are taken at 2.30 pm and the inn closes for the day at 4 pm. Draught beers offered include Bass, London Pride, IPA and Sussex ales with a good selection of wine by the glass or bottle. The pub is very popular with locals and visitors alike as it makes the perfect starting point for a stroll around this pretty area. On the day I called one of those light mists that sometimes cover the foot of the North Downs was just lifting, giving the pub a somewhat mystical look. Later, as the sun broke through, I sat outside with my lunch in the shade of a tree in the secluded garden. Because of the pub's popularity it is essential to reserve a table if you wish to eat a meal here (bar snacks available without booking). Telephone: 01483 421158.

The Walk

① From the Withies Inn walk out to the lane and turn right along it, heading away from the B3000. At a junction of lanes by a small triangle of grass turn left and in 20 yards go right onto a well-walked footpath. Continue through woodland to reach a stile which you cross. Keep to this pleasant path as it skirts a couple of fields and brings you to a junction of paths by a concrete farm track.

② Ignore a stile on your right but cross the stile ahead of you and turn leftwards along the farm track. Follow the directional arrows as you go to the left of a large barn and pass by the rear of the old buildings of Coneycroft Farm to reach a lane. (A well worthwhile detour of 100 yards leftwards down the lane brings you to the cemetery and the magnificent Watts Chapel.) The way is rightwards along the lane for a short distance to reach a sandy track alongside the Watts Gallery to your right signposted 'North Downs

PLACE OF INTEREST NEARBY

The **Watts Gallery** displays the work of the famous Victorian artist. Open Monday, Tuesday, Friday and Sunday from 2 pm to 6 pm (5 pm in winter); Wednesday and Saturday 11 am to 1 pm and 2 pm to 6 pm; Thursday closed. Telephone: 01483 810235.

Pleasant paths make for easy walking.

Way'. You may wish to visit the Watts Gallery or the delightful tea rooms that are open from 10.30 am to 5.30 pm every day.

③ Our route is along the sandy North Downs Way and over the fields on your left will be seen the slopes of the Hog's Back. The track eventually brings you to farm buildings where sometimes there is a display of farm produce for sale. I purchased a small bag of new potatoes and $1/2$ dozen newly laid eggs when I last passed this way and very nice they were

indeed. The track narrows here and continues up a rise between sandy banks.

④ After going over the crest of the rise a junction of paths is met and our route follows the narrow downhill path to your right. At the end of the path continue ahead on the tarmac lane and pass Polsted Manor. Press on along the lane to return to the junction of lanes by the small triangle of grass. Keep to the left here and very soon the Withies Inn and the end of the stroll will be reached.

Shamley Green
The Red Lion

MAP: OS LANDRANGER 186 (GR 032439) **WALK 26** **DISTANCE:** $2^3/_4$ MILES

DIRECTIONS TO START: SHAMLEY GREEN IS 4 MILES SOUTH OF GUILDFORD ON THE B2128. **PARKING:** IN THE PUB CAR PARK OR AROUND THE VILLAGE GREEN.

This pretty rural community, once known as Shamble Lea, is spread out around a large green divided by roads that separate the pond from the cricket pitch and another that unusually divides the crease from the northern boundary. Attractive houses, some dating back to the 16th century, surround this agreeable spot from where our country stroll starts. The route first heads westwards along a pleasant lane and through fields where we cross the river Wey South Branch and the remains of the short lived Wey and Arun Canal. Turning south for a while we follow the Wey South Path along an old disused railway bed that traces the route of the canal it helped to close. Oak and birch trees that have grown along the protected embankment give good shade here on hot summer days. Soon we re-cross the river and continue over more scenic fields on our return to the village where we rejoin the green near its charming duck pond.

The Red Lion

Situated opposite the cricket pitch in this lovely village is the pretty Red Lion pub. Once a coaching inn, the Grade II listed building makes the perfect spot for refreshment before or after your stroll. The opening hours here are some of the longest I've come across and if you are an early bird then you are able to purchase a good cup of coffee from 7 am throughout the week and from the unearthly hour of 8 am on Sundays. During licensing hours there is a good selection of liquid refreshment of a different kind that includes Young's, Flowers, Abbot Ale, Murphy's, Carlsberg, 4X and Lowenbrau.

A warm summer sun was shinning when I sat at a table on the patio overlooking the green. Nearby a horse was tethered and was patiently awaiting its master who was seeking liquid refreshment. A quiet game of cricket was being played out on the green opposite and I have to admit that had I not already completed my stroll it would have taken the strength of the horse to get me to leave my seat, especially after consuming a large home-cooked meal. You will find a nice selection of bar food including children-sized alternatives and a vegetarian choice plus an à la carte menu which all goes to make booking a table essential at this very popular pub. Telephone: 01483 892202.

The Walk

① With the Red Lion behind you, cross the B2128 and continue along the left side

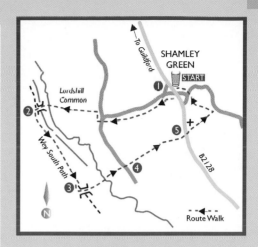

of the cricket pitch. At the end of the green maintain direction ahead along Hullbrook Lane until a road junction is met. Go right here for a few yards and then left on a path beside a house. After passing the garden our way continues between fields and crosses the river Wey South Branch. Soon, at a bridge go left to meet the bed of a now defunct railway.

② Press on leftwards along this very pleasant track that forms a part of the long distance Wey South Path. Protected from the ravages of the plough, this ribbon of woodland is a haven for wildlife and plenty can be seen and heard along here. For a short while the remains of the Wey and Arun Canal can be viewed through the trees on your left. Built in 1816 the

PLACE OF INTEREST NEARBY
Winkworth Arboretum is in a wonderful setting with tree and shrub covered hills reflected in the mirror-like lake. Open all year during daylight hours it can be found on the B2130 south of Godalming. Telephone: 01483 208477

Playing cricket on the village green.

canal created a link with the south coast but as road and rail links improved, the traffic on the canal waned and it closed after little more than fifty years.

③ At an overhead bridge turn right up steps to reach it and then go left along a farm track. Within yards you pass lonely Fanesbridge Cottage where all signs of the canal that once ran along the left side of the house have disappeared. Soon two field gates are met and you should go through the right-hand one and head for a small bridge where you re-cross the river on a sweeping bend. Press on along the path signed as 'GW' (Greensands Way).

④ When a tarmac drive is met go diagonally right and continue ahead along a waymarked path that leads you between fields with rural views and finally reaches a road.

⑤ The way is ahead on the enclosed footpath opposite where you soon cross fields with magnificent views. Finally when a narrow path is met by a hedgerow turn left along it and follow its course as it skirts a field before passing between gardens. The path ends alongside a picturesque house where you should now go diagonally right to meet the village pond and the Red Lion beyond.

Walliswood
The Scarlett Arms

MAP: OS LANDRANGER 187 (GR 119382)   **WALK 27**   **DISTANCE:** 3 MILES

DIRECTIONS TO START: WALLISWOOD IS 2½ MILES SOUTH-EAST OF EWHURST AND JUST SHORT OF THE SUSSEX BORDER. **PARKING:** IN THE PARKING AREA OPPOSITE THE PUB OR ALONG THE ROAD.

The village names of Oakwoodhill, Forest Green and Walliswood tell you that this part of Surrey was carved out of the great Wealden forest that until a few centuries ago thickly covered much of the county. Starting life as small isolated forest settlements these little hamlets remain off the beaten track and fortunately are bypassed by the A29 coast road a couple of miles away to the east.

Our lovely circuit starts off in a westerly direction before soon turning north along an enchanting old green lane that leads us along a ribbon of woodland. As the route swings around to the east we have splendid views over pastures to Leith Hill. Soon we pass through tiny Mayes Green where even at walking pace a blink means you could miss it. Heading back now we pass through fine woodland where an assortment of homes are dotted among the trees.

The Scarlett Arms

Originally built around four hundred years ago as workers' cottages, this lovely building was converted into a public house three hundred years later which goes some way to explaining why, during winter, there are two roaring fires in the snug bar area. Mind your head on the low oak beams that exude atmosphere, as does the flagstone floor. During the summer months, tables under cheerfully coloured umbrellas are set out in the front garden and help to make this one of Surrey's prettiest pubs.

Traditional pub hours of 11 am to 2.30 pm and 5.30 pm to 11 pm for weekdays and Saturdays apply here while on Sundays they are 12 noon to 3 pm and 7 pm to 10.30 pm. Tradition extends to the banning of children under fourteen entering the bar although they are most welcome in the garden. Booking is advisable if you wish to avail yourself of the superb home-made food that is cooked to order. From the pumps come Sussex and Tanglefoot bitters plus cider, Guinness and lager, but if they prove too strong to sup before your stroll you will be pleased to find that King & Barnes Mild is also on offer as is a selection of wine. Telephone: 01306 627243.

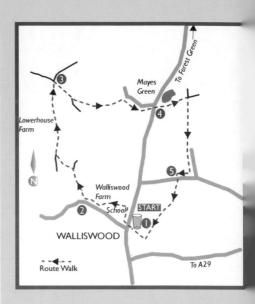

The Walk

① With your back to the pub go rightwards along the road to a small green. Turn left along a drive and pass the left side of a garage showroom. Keep ahead through a kissing gate and maintain direction over a couple of stiles and through a gate. Soon pass between farm buildings and through a five bar gate to reach a lane where you should now turn right.

② Immediately after a bungalow on your right, turn right on a footpath along a driveway. At the crest of a rise go left over a stile and continue along an enclosed path to reach a tranquil wildflower meadow. Go diagonally left to meet a stile and enter woodland. Keep to the well-trodden path to soon meet a T-

PLACE OF INTEREST NEARBY

The **Hannah Peschar Sculpture Garden** displays over 80 sculptures among the plants and can be found in Standon Lane halfway between Walliswood and Ockley. Open May to October on Fridays and Saturdays from 11 am to 6 pm and Sundays from 2 pm to 5 pm. Telephone: 01306 627269.

On the route.

junction with a wide track. Turn right here and stay on this track until a driveway is met with a lane beyond.

③ Turn right on a footpath along the driveway and pass stables. At a right bend in the drive cross a stile on your left and go diagonally right on an indistinct path to the top corner of the field. Go through a five bar gate and continue ahead. Cross a stile and press on ahead with views to the North Downs and Leith Hill tower just visible amongst the trees on the skyline. At a small road junction continue ahead and stay on this lane until it meets a T-junction with a larger road.

④ This is the tiny hamlet of Mayes Green with its well-manicured green and small pond with its interesting display of water plants. Our way is ahead along a rough track that runs past this picturesque scene. At a junction of tracks turn right on a wide track that leads you through a ribbon of woodland with a golf course to your left. Eventually the track meets a lane where you continue ahead to meet a road junction.

⑤ Go rightwards along the road and just before a house on your right go left on a path through woodland. Soon at a waymark sign bear left and in 20 yards or so bear right on a narrower path. Quite soon our route passes between a couple of bungalows in woodland clearings. Cross a drive and maintain direction, keeping ahead at a second drive. The path crosses a stream and meets a T-junction with a small brook with houses beyond. Turn right here alongside the brook and pass through a kissing gate to meet a road where, by going right, you will come to the Scarlett Arms and the end of the stroll.

Newdigate
The Six Bells

MAP: OS LANDRANGER 187 (GR 198421)   **WALK 28**   **DISTANCE:** 3¾ MILES

DIRECTIONS TO START: NEWDIGATE IS 6 MILES SOUTH OF DORKING AND 2 MILES EAST OF THE A24 AT BEARE GREEN. THE SIX BELLS IS AT THE SOUTHERN END OF THE VILLAGE. **PARKING:** IN THE PUB CAR PARK OR ALONG THE ROAD.

Down in the Weald near the Sussex border is the scattered village of Newdigate, once described as 'the loneliest place in Surrey'. The Wealden forest disappeared from here centuries ago but some of its large boughs can still be seen in the old timber-framed cottages around the area, but by far the most significant are the massive 500 year old timbers that support the bell tower of St Peter's church.

From here our route lies over pleasant fields and along farm tracks where we pass a couple of charming ponds. Strolling along field edges with summertime hedgerows bedecked with wild roses we reach the small settlement of Cudworth where we pass an immense barn with timbers a century older than those of St Peter's. The route takes us past the moat of Cudworth Manor which in part dates back to the 13th century but is now much modernised. Continuing along quiet lanes the way brings us back to the church, the Six Bells and the end of the stroll.

The Six Bells

What a joy and a surprise this fine village freehouse is! Dating back to the 17th century, rumour abounds that it was once used by smugglers on their way from the coast to London and the remains of a tunnel where they stashed their contraband French brandy is to be found in the cellar. Nowadays the more traditional choice of refreshments includes Young's, Sussex and Pedigree bitters plus Greene King IPA. During winter ensconce yourself into a comfortable seat and be warmed by the roaring fire in the inglenook fireplace as you contemplate the old pictures and photographs adorning the walls that depict Newdigate's past. Of course you may well visit during the summer months and sit at an umbrella-shaded table in the very pleasant garden where children can play on the swings and climbing frame.

Bar food is available from 12 noon to 2.30 pm and 7 pm to 9.30 pm Monday to Saturday and on Sunday from 12 noon to 2.30 pm only. However, should you want something more elaborate then I can highly recommend the self-contained restaurant which is a must for the food connoisseur. Here you will find an exquisite choice of dishes from the table d'hôte and à la carte menus that will suit every palate. The restaurant is open six days a week for lunches and dinner and booking is recommended. Telephone: 01306 631276.

The Walk

① With the pub at your back, turn right along the road and soon go right on a signposted path along the edge of two fields. At the end of the second field cross a stile and planked bridge and keep ahead. Ignore a stile in 180 yards but cross a half-hidden stile 150 yards later to meet a farm track at the far side of the field.

② Turn left along the track and pass an idyllic pond where I was treated to the sight of a heron fishing while a love-struck toad called out loudly for a mate. Keep ahead on the track until it reaches Green's Farm.

③ At a junction of tracks by a fingerpost turn right and pass a small pond. Go between farm buildings and immediately

PLACE OF INTEREST NEARBY

Dorking Museum has a selection of exhibits ranging from a stuffed 'Dorking cockerel' to farm implements. Found in West Street, this small museum is open on Wednesdays and Thursdays from 2 pm to 5 pm and on Saturday from 10 am to 5 pm. Telephone: 01306 876591.

The shingle spire of St Peter's church, Newdigate.

meet and cross a stile t
a farm track.

④ Go ahead along th
track and pass by the gat
to Home Farm. When th
track bends sharply righ
go through a narro
metal gate to your lef
Continue through
second gate and at
third, cross a stile to th
right of it and continu
diagonally right over
meadow to reach idylli
ponds.

⑤ Go between the
ponds on a track and a
it bends sharply left g
right over a stile t
continue through a field
where you pass by the
end of the pond. Cross a
bridge and stile and g
over a field to a stile
hidden in the hedge in
the far corner. Follow the
left edge of a meadow to
reach a large garden. Go
ahead along the right-
hand edge of the well-
manicured garden to pass
stables and reach a track; go left along it.

go left and cross a stile ahead of you. Keep
to the left side of the field for 80 yards and
then cross a stile to your left. Proceed
diagonally right to meet and cross a stile in
the far corner. Maintain direction over the
next two fields to meet a road alongside
Tanhurst Farm. Turn right here and then
left into the driveway of Ockley Lodge. In
20 yards cross a stile on your right and
remain roughly parallel with the drive to

⑥ When the large barn at Cudworth is
reached, turn left along Cudworth Lane
and pass the moated manor house. Keep
to this lane until it meets with a tarmac
road. Go right along the road and at a
junction by Oakfield House, turn left to
pass a pond and soon reach the Six Bells
pub and the end of the stroll.

Grayswood
The Wheatsheaf Inn

MAP: OS LANDRANGER 186 (GR 916346)　　**WALK 29**　　**DISTANCE:** 3¼ MILES

DIRECTIONS TO START: GRAYSWOOD SITS ASTRIDE THE A286 JUST 1 MILE NORTH-EAST OF HASLEMERE.
PARKING: IN THE PUB CAR PARK OR ALONG LOWER ROAD BY THE CRICKET GREEN.

Passing motorists, with their eyes transfixed on the twisting A286, see very little of the small hamlet of Grayswood as they speed on their way to and from Haslemere and beyond. Many of its houses lay hidden down small lanes behind the beautifully kept green. The cricket pitch is magnificent and has an ancient spreading oak growing well within its southern boundary while on the northern border is one of the nicest village halls I have ever seen. Across the busy main road is the startling little parish church that was built in 1901 by a Swedish architect, and its Scandinavian ancestry shows.

The stroll passes this pleasant setting as we set out along a quiet road that brings us to open fields with pastoral views. As the route circles Frillinghurst Wood we cross more fields and enter quiet woodland to reach High Prestwick Farm. From here our return brings us across an elevated meadow where the views towards Hindhead are quite outstanding.

The Wheatsheaf Inn

If you visit during the summer months you cannot fail to be impressed by the wonderful display of hanging baskets that adorn the front veranda. This lovely freehouse offers the visitor a warm and friendly atmosphere and its delightful garden includes a small children's play area.

As well as a comprehensive list of wines, you can enjoy a wide range of beers from the pumps, including London Pride, ESB, Harveys Sussex Bitter, Stella Artois, Carlsberg and Guinness, also Strongbow cider. Opening hours are the traditional 11 am to 3 pm and 6 pm to 11 pm throughout the week while on Sundays they are 12 noon to 3 pm and 6 pm to 10.30 pm. There is an excellent selection of freshly prepared meals served to an award-winning standard that can either be eaten in the bar or in the splendid surroundings of the small dining room. The choice of food when I called ranged from a variety of sandwiches, which included fresh salmon and cucumber contained between thickly cut slices of speckled bloomer, and ploughman's to – from the main menu – a more substantial meal of rib eye steak with tomatoes, mushrooms and garlic butter. It is always worth checking out the blackboard for the daily 'specials' too. Booking is necessary for sit down meals. Telephone: 01428 644440.

The Walk

① From the Wheatsheaf walk downhill along the A286 to reach the village green

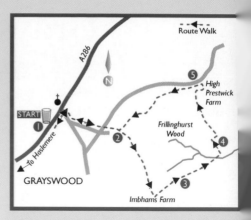

where you should now turn right and continue along Lower Road. Ignore turnings to your right. At a T-junction with Clammer Hill, go ahead along a rough track opposite.

② When the track finally ends by a gate, keep ahead on a narrower path and cross a field. Soon you pass through a narrow strip of woodland and continue over a second field. Go over a third field and at the far side, with the roof of Imbhams Farm visible to your right, turn left along the field edge on a wide grassy track with a hedgerow on the right.

③ At the end of the field keep ahead on a grassy track and at a fork go left. As you meet a wider track bear left along it to reach a field. Follow the left-hand edge and when opposite a barn look out for a half-hidden stile on your left. Cross this

PLACE OF INTEREST NEARBY

Haslemere Museum in the High Street started life in 1888 as the private collection of Sir Jonathan Hutchinson. Open to the public on Tuesday to Saturday, 10 am to 5 pm from April to October and 10 am to 4 pm from November to March. Telephone: 01428 642112.

All Saints' church opposite the village green.

hillock look out for a stile hidden in the field edge to your left. Cross this and maintain direction on a narrow woodland path that eventually brings you to a field edge. Press on up the right-hand side of the field and go through a gate beside a scenic summerhouse. Keep ahead and pass between the barn and farm cottages of High Prestwick Farm to reach a road.

⑤ Turn left here and within yards of passing pretty Damson Cottage go left on a narrow public footpath. Persevere along this scrappy little path and it will bring you to open fields where you maintain direction to the top of an incline. The scenery is superb here as you gaze over the valley towards Hindhead. Go through a field gate where you will be confronted by three others. Pass through the gate to your right and continue diagonally right across the centre of the field towards houses, aiming for a stile in the far edge which you cross. Go ahead over a tarmac track and proceed along a path opposite where you pass stables. After passing the side of a large garden you will meet up with the track walked earlier. Turn right here and retrace your steps back to the Wheatsheaf and the end of the stroll.

and almost immediately the path goes downhill and crosses a tributary of the river Arun. Continue up the other side to meet a stile at a field edge. Cross the stile and turn left to meet another in 30 yards which you cross and enter woodland.

④ After 40 yards turn right on an uphill path through trees to meet a T-junction. Turn right here and very soon by a gate go left on a narrow footpath. Cross a stile and continue along the left-hand side of a field that offers panoramic views over the adjoining countryside. After going over a

Dunsfold
The Sun Inn

MAP: OS LANDRANGER 186 (GR 005363)   **WALK 30**   **DISTANCE:** 1½ MILES

DIRECTIONS TO START: DUNSFOLD IS 6 MILES SOUTH OF GUILDFORD. FOLLOW SIGNS FROM THE A281 A NANHURST CROSSROADS. **PARKING:** AROUND THE VILLAGE GREEN BY THE SUN INN.

This spread-out little community down near the Sussex border is unusual in that its church is half a mile away from the huge green where old cottages, pub and duck pond make up the indistinct core of the village. After leaving the green behind the route soon crosses the infant river Arun and then follows its banks for a short distance where we discover a Holy Well once believed to cure eye disorders. Nearby we pass the lovely old church of Saint Mary and All Saints. The church is 13th century but something much older grows near the porch – a yew tree now hollow and in poor condition that dates back to the Norman Conquest. The small settlement that has grown up around the church is called Church Green and it would be hard to find a nicer setting in all of Surrey. Leaving this pretty place we follow quiet lanes to bring us back to the Sun Inn and the end of our stroll.